WRITING (FOR BEER MONEY)

The Advice and Self-Indulgence of a Successful Writer and a Highly Unsuccessful Author...

DR. DAVID J WINTERS, PHD

{Subgenre:Publishers}

CONTENTS

Also by David J. Winters	v
Preface (to a Patently Cheap Cash-Grab)	ix

PART I: WHO'S EVEN WRITING THIS?

Who Am I?	3

PART II: SOME STRAIGHTFORWARD ADVICE

Novelize Your Script or Script Your Novel?	11
Batch Publishing and Avoiding the Sophomore Curse (an Experiment)	22
Some Single Story-Thread Novels are like Movies, Some are like Cable TV Seasons...	30
Gettin' Precious	35
A Non-Exhaustive, Non-Threatening, (Non-Professional) List of Ways Reclusive Writers can Polish their Work and Stay Motivated	43

PART III: MURDER MYSTERY WRITING ADVICE

Let Em get Away with It... Then Don't (1 MOD 1)	59
Let Em get Away With it... Then Don't (2 MOD 1)	80

PART IIII: CHATGPTHEATER

Jaws	99
Ghostbusters	116

The Terminator	130
Big Trouble in Little China	150

PART IIIII: GEMINI CAN HAS LITZERATURE?

Nineteen Eighty-Four	169
Crime and Punishment	178

PART IIIIII: GROK AROUND THE CLOCK

Born in the USA	189

PART ING: IS SUCH SWEET SORROW...

My Latest	201
A Turn of Praise	204
About the Author	209

ALSO BY DAVID J. WINTERS

BEDSIDE MANNER

Nurse-and-union-leader *turned* homicide-detective, Eminence Gray, uses her gifts of empathy and emotional labor to catch the most vicious of West Brandon's killers. Em's ability to maintain this skillset will be put to the ultimate test when the highest-profile murder case her department has ever faced falls right into her lap. Add to Em's troubles a corrupt executive from her union days, back and up to old tricks, and it might just be Eminence Gray requiring a little *bedside manner*... or a lot.

INTERVENTIONISM

Roger Jech doesn't have any superpowers, but he has a super ability: harm him, harm yourself in equal measure. Hit him with a right hook, your jaw breaks. Shoot him in the head, your brains blow out the back of you. Drop him in a war zone, your enemies kill themselves killing him. Jech's a weapon to the wrong people and a savior to the right, but before he can become the latter, he must learn to harness his gift before it becomes his curse.

THE TAKING OF SHALE CITY

Shale City has seen better days. First, the dam burst, flooding out the town's iron mine. Then, local officials shut down the shipping and courier services, the only thing keeping Shale City hanging on... It was all the mayor of Shale could do to fight off the more 'legitimate' of sleazeballs trying to destroy her city, but now it seems as though some other kind of sleazeball force is encroaching upon her town, set on putting the final nail in its coffin...

Writing (For Beer Money)
Copyright © 2025 by David J. Winters
All rights reserved.

No part of this book may be reproduced in any form or by any electronic or mechanical means, including information storage and retrieval systems, without written permission from the author, except for the use of brief quotations in a book review.

This is a work of nonfiction for the most part. Of the fictional elements, all of the characters, organizations, and events portrayed are not real as far as I, and the AIs who love me, know. (And, by 'as far as we know' I mean we all know sufficiently well that they are not real... That's how far we know baby!)

ISBN 9781068863691 (paperback) | ISBN 9781068863684 (hardcover) | ISBN 9781068863684 (electronic book)

{SubGenre : Publishers}
www.subgenrepublishers.com

For MAD Magazine

PREFACE (TO A PATENTLY CHEAP CASH-GRAB)
(THAT WILL ALMOST CERTAINLY NOT GENERATE ANY CASH...)

> *I'm going to throw all of my 'writing on writing' newsletters into a book and call it advice and try to publish it. Here's a rough draft of the preface for that book:*
>
> — BETTER AUTHORS THAN ME TALKING TO THEIR AGENTS... SO WHY NOT ME TOO GODDAMN IT!

Ahem.

I am a highly successful writer. I've written things. Many things. I'm writing *this* right now. My stuff's often grammatically correct! That's technically all it takes and more, QED.

I am also a highly highly unsuccessful author. I have written and published a lot given the short amount of time I had to write it, put it up for sale, and make the very little money I made doing so. I published five books in one year for crying out loud! More on that later...

Now, by *unsuccessful author* I don't mean to say I'm a *failed author*. I think to be a failed author you would need catch the attention of a sufficient number of people who purchase and/or discuss your works and then either:

1. See your increased exposure just fall off a cliff of absolutely no one wanting to touch any further of your publications and see this happen suddenly where from this point on your level of success will never progress beyond *modest* (causing you to forget about ever seeing *maximal* as you won't even get to *moderate*).

or,

2. See this increased exposure only result in a tremendous amount of negative attention, leading to your body of work becoming a laughing stock among general readers, critics, and publishers or, alternatively, find yourself beloved by modern-day English professors. Note that these scenarios are equivalent in effect: *i.e.* your reputation will be in tatters and you'll forever be a joke in the industry.

or,

3. Both of the above, making this list no longer of the either/or variety as we now have a third option.

or,

4. Something else that ensures your lack of bankability and respect while also ensuring this

list *definitely unassailably* no longer of the either/or variety (and vague in addition!).

No, I'm definitely not a failed author but at this point I would love to be as I've likely relegated myself to the massively growing pile of *unsuccessful authors* forever, where being a *failed author* would at least have meant making some money for some amount of time...

No, I'm just your average run-of-the-mill unsuccessful author. But why?

WHY?

It's not because I'm awful (I'm mediocre at least). It's not because I'm lacking in self-indulgence (just look at this preface). It's not because I'll be beloved *only* not in my lifetime. It's not because people only want to read lurid romance novels featuring AI hardbodies groping each other on the covers or, in lieu of that, 'Young Adult' fantasy fiction novels (numbered 37 of a series of 82). It's not because of a Marxist, identitarian, critical theory, intersectionalist, post-structuralist take-over of the publishing industry by middle-aged suburban women with MFAs (whatever all that means...). It's because of... Wait a minute... What's the 'it' I'm looking for again?

Gimme a second...

Ah yes... It's because *I'm too damn reclusive for my own good!* (At least that's what I'll be going with...)

You see...

The *day* of writers like J.D. Salinger and Thomas Pynchon writing solely down on the farm and never having to see the light of a day's worth of photons reflected off the shiny, clammy, pallorous complexions of fellow writers, editors, publishing company executives, devoted readers, etc. is over. And I say the 'day' is over *singular* as the extroverts of the world were never going to allow this trend of *people with good ideas sharing these ideas free of having to breathe each others' air* to continue for more than twenty-four hours.

They'd be damned if their precious *physical proximity* was going to be threatened by the slight accommodation of people not so desperate for attention (and to be attentive) that the quarantine is scarier than the disease... of society man!

They'd be damned damned if us introverts would ever be allowed to just dummy-up in a hole somewhere and live! There'll be no such accommodation for those of the world not so desperate to gratify their social predilections that they'd demand a constant audience to hear (and speak) every single thing that should ever deign to pass through their collective heads.

No, extroverts would be so so damned if they'd ever let their world become a place allowing more than *anybody* the ability to work successfully in relative seclusion.

Extroverts rule the world and what they desire most is a world of people always at hand, keeping nothing to themselves, closely.

Am I bitter? Short answer: yes. Long answer: Yessiree Bob.

But more on this later...

So, for now, you'll all have to settle for doing things best done alone in massive office suites, conference halls, large block book stores and - god-forbid - a portable yurt in the backyard of the COO's house on a half-Friday... And more!

You'll all have to settle.

But not me baby! And that's why I suck.

This 'I'm too reclusive for my own good' hypothesis is seriously what I'm going with y'all.

BUT WHAT ABOUT THE OBVIOUS?

But I guess there's also the fact that people don't read much these days (where *not reading at all* implies *not reading much*).

Yes, by refusing to network I'm like a man without a microphone seeking work as an announcer on AM radio. Even if I had this microphone, chances are virtually none of making any kind of living whatsoever as who the hell even listens to any kind of radio anymore? Just my parents I guess and they're already subsidizing my ~~failed~~ unsuccessful writing career. But, enough of my mixing my metaphors with the bleak realities that spawned them...

OH WELL

Oh well. What's a writer of too few necessary conditions met to be successful to do?

Write a book of writing advice, naturally! Even better: just mash together a bunch of hardly-read articles on writing advice and try to pass it off as a coherent well-thought-out whole!

So where do I start? With a preface, of course! A chapter that tries to tie all of the following disjointed works together according to a common theme and goal. And that preface is thus:

> **Step back from the book a little and take it all in.*

And that goal-oriented theme is this:

PREFACE (TO A PATENTLY CHEAP CASH-GRAB)

Writing successfully.

What am I supposed to do with just this concept? you might be asking. That's the problem. A theme is just an idea that recurs throughout a creative work and that's exactly what I've represented above, which is trivial. Obviously the theme of any writing advice manual is 'Writing successfully'. So, in addition to a goal-oriented theme, I need a thesis *better* a hook. How about this:

> *This is a book of writing advice that's actually quite good at times from a writer of some merit but far too little sociability to do anything other than dump his written works all over the internet and now this book; a writer who's hoping this work of non-fiction will stand a better chance than his works of fiction at catching flies without having to employ anything other than the same a-social methods that caused his fictional works to not sell, who's also hoping to pass onto you - the reader - some advice that will help you - at-minimum - become the kind of writer you always wanted to be for yourself (and a small but dedicated fan-base) but maybe even become the kind of writer who'll break into the industry and make a real splash!*

That was seriously a single sentence! Had to use a semi-colon though...

That's the intent behind all this: help writers like me by providing them with legit writing advice as well as heartening anecdotes about becoming an author. An author who's seen very few sales, admittedly, but whose advice is still valid.

Therefore, this isn't a book on the *business* of writing,

only the *writing* of writing. I may have failed to succeed at conquering the business aspect, but I certainly succeeded at conquering the writing aspect. My stories have been told but not bought, but they've been told and I couldn't have done it without me. With my help, you'll be able to do the same. But the better news is, even if you have just a shred of an ability to work with others, you may just be able to make that sweet sweet living.

If not, at the very least, you'll have paid for this book.
Enjoy!

Dr. David Joseph Winters, PhD

PART I: WHO'S EVEN WRITING THIS?

WHO INDEED?

WHO AM I?

FIVE BOOKS. ONE SHORT STORY. ONE YEAR. THAT'S WHO I AM!

In all seriousness...

Who am I? I'm a failed school teacher later a failed logician. Logician is where the 'Dr.' and 'PhD' in the author credit come from. Seriously, I'm a logician just like Bertrand Russell only real. Like Sherlock Holmes only Spock...

Why'd I fail at teaching and being logical for a living? Let's start with teaching second, and logic after that.

I failed at being a logician because the last thing I figured out about being a logician (that kinda disqualifies me from being a logician) is that the last thing the world wants is a logician.

Wanna get a job teaching logic at a university? Better have a degree in marxist feminist ethics, culinary arts, puppetry, or something else equally pertinent... Wanna charge somebody with denying the antecedent? Do it if and only if you want to enter into a fruitless discussion of the difference between *if* and *only if*... Wanna throw a consistency operator into your predicate calculus so you can violate the law of contradiction without explosion only to be scoffed at by classicists? Do it with the knowledge that classical logicians *will not* scoff at you because there ain't no logicians no'mo' because the last thing the world wants is a logician!

Am I bitter? I already said I was in the preface! And that was an all-encompassing bitterness!

But I regress...

The last thing the world wants is a logician. I'm a logician. You figure the rest out (but not too quickly or you'll be in the same boat as me).

Yup, everyone hates a logician. So, naturally, everyone loves teachers[1].

Being a logician disqualified me from being a teacher. That's the logic of it. But *you were a teacher before you were a logician?* I hear you asking? Fine, you got me. But just like educators hate logicians, they also hate people who think education is a waste of time[2] but who only go into ed programs because teaching is easy money and said program was close enough to his girlfriend at the time to allow him to both keep shacking up with her and impress her with all the easy money to come only to have her dump me just a week into classes...

I never stood a chance.

So who am I really? I'm all those failed things above but I'm also *not* a failed author, just like the preface and subtitle say.

But enough talk of subtitles. Let's talk about titles![3]

---

1. Speaking of denying the antecedent...
2. *But you went back to school to become a logician...*
3. In all of my many years of editing this book I still read this sentence as 'Let's talk about titties!'. (You know, like the boobs?)

PART I: WHO'S EVEN WRITING THIS?

The parenthetical aside in the title of this book is,

> *For Beer Money*

The rest of the title is just,

> *Writing*

Altogether[4] that gets us,

> *For Beer Money Writing*[5]

The concept of writing for beer money is in reference to the self-indulgent 'memoir' portion of this masterpiece and not the advice portion. I don't intend to advise you on how to write for beer money. That's what I did and I wouldn't advise that.

Now, to be clear, I didn't write *for* beer money. That is, writing for beer money wasn't my intent. However, what I was paid by those gracious enough to buy my stuff amounted to just enough money to buy a year's worth of beer.

I published 5 books from January 1st 2024 to January 1st 2025. That's 2 medium-chunky novels, 1 novel proper, 1 li'l-cutey (borderline novella), and 1 novella. I wrote a sizable enough short story too. All this adds up to about 1250 pages of a standardly formatted paperback.

You could also describe how much I wrote thus:

- I wrote the equivalent of 8.34 Louis L'Amours.

---

4. Note that 'altogether' is 'all together' all together.
5. **No parenthesis for emphasis.*

- You could say if you had to (and you do): I wrote 1 Clavell.
- That's about 2 Kings?
- And then there were 6 Christies.
- Or, how 'bout this: I wrote an *UNDEFINED* number of Poes... Because! Edgar Allan Poe famously never wrote a novel and *UNDEFINED* is what you get when you divide my 1250 pages by the 0 pages of your average Poe novel.
- I also wrote an *UNDEFINED* number of Cleroy Baxleys (Cleroy *non-famously* never wrote a novel).
- Interestingly, I wrote -3 Ellises... Because a negative number is what you get when you divide by *Less Than Zero. Whah! Whah!*
- Lastly, although I'm more of a Milton Friedman kinda guy, I wrote .3254 Rands.

I writed, forma-tted, and (as with everything I put on the page) beautifully edited all of my books to perfection. I then published them under my own label SubGenre Publishers (who else would?).

All of the writing, editing, formatting, and publishing was far easier than achieving what was necessary to adequately market my works. However, marketing my books was far easier than anything else I did. This is no contradiction baby. You see, although it *is* much harder to adequately market a book than it is to write one, the marketing of my books was done nowhere close to adequate.

To recapitulate everything perfectly succinctly and articulately: my approach to all this nonsense was exactly as Frank Sinatra described all those guys who covered a certain of his songs:

PART I: WHO'S EVEN WRITING THIS?

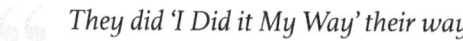 *They did 'I Did it My Way' their way*

I did it my way and I got the *Community Inn Beer Vendor* receipts to prove it!

All this almost over with, here's the dirty little secret about my writing and the monetizing of it: I would have happily taken more than four bucks a week for it. Hell, I'd have taken a living for it. Don't judge me!

Now *that* was my true intent.

Don't judge me!

What started out as me just wanting to get a few of the stories I had deep down inside me on the page (and made available for public consumption), ended with me getting a few of the stories I had deep down inside me on the page (and made available for public consumption). And, I never could have done it without doing that.

So, what's next? Oh, I have a few irons up my sleeve and they all involve getting a real job for the next 40 years, dying, and not being appreciated in my own time or any time.

All irons up my sleeve *but one* I should say! The real one (the real iron) involves me becoming a best-selling author by next week (with a net worth comparable to JK Rowlings' if she invested it in Apple in 1999) and then living forever! *All because* y'all bought this book and were then spurred on to buy the rest of my books as well as petition your governments to write into law the buying of the film rights to my stuff after a long drawn out series of bidding wars between studio heads (fighting with knives), leading to the purchase of said rights for 10% of the film's projected 1.5 billion dollar budget which is double the 5% cap!

And I couldn't have done any of this without your

support, so, from the bottom of my heart I say to you: *get to work.*

PART II: SOME STRAIGHTFORWARD ADVICE

THE SECOND-LEAST JACKASSERY-LADEN/SMARTASSERY-LADEN, SECTION OF THIS BOOK (FEEL FREE TO SKIP...)

NOVELIZE YOUR SCRIPT OR SCRIPT YOUR NOVEL?

WHAT OUGHT COME FIRST WITH MULTIPLE MEDIA FORMATTING

I'm going to start this chapter assuming for the sake of argument:

> *If you want to break into fiction writing markets in this day and age, you won't.*

I'm going to continue this chapter assuming for the sake of argument:

> *If you want to break into fiction writing markets in this day and age, you really ought put your story out there in as many media formats as possible.*

Do the screenplay. Do the novel. Do the graphic novel. Do the TV pilot, the play, the video game, the board game, the T-shirt. Publish your work in as many formats as you can since *for one*, you'll open up more avenues of interest in your work and *for two*, the hardest part is conceiving-of and reifying the story anyway. Everything that follows after establishing your story is rote adaptation... Almost[1].

I think it's all rote if you write the novel first[2]. I wrote three feature screenplays before novelizing all of them (really, novelizing two and *novella-izing* the third). I wish I had done this in reverse, for three reasons:

1. By the time I got back to my scripts in order to novelize them, I had lost 'the movie'.
2. If I had written the novel first, all desirable details would have been on the page and I wouldn't have been so tempted to bloat out the script with 'my vision'.
3. It was too tempting to just copy-and-paste the script from Final Draft to Word then change the margins and add quotation marks (and what that leaves is not a novel).

Writing the novel first would have prevented these issues (and not caused others). Here's why...

LOSING THE MOVIE

The scripts I've since novelized are called *Interventionism*,

---

1. The graphic novel notwithstanding, as pencilling, inking, and colouring constitute a particularly daunting task for a person who's only ever typed. But, if you're doing the graphic novel in addition to many other formats, you're likely not doing the artwork yourself and are at least halfway towards some sort of plan for commissioning (or partnering with) an action comics artist/artists. For you the writer then, writing the graphic novel is a much more straightforward matter of adapting a novel to a comics script.
2. Rote if you want it. There is always the freedom to include/exclude scenes, reorganize scenes, rewrite scenes, add unwritten scenes, etc. But, with the novel, you have the complete blueprint, maximal materials, and the structure.

PART II: SOME STRAIGHTFORWARD ADVICE

Bedside Manner, and *Scarcity*. As scripts the former two were bloated as hell (~160 pages each) but that didn't mean there wasn't a world of description left off the page. It's a courtesy, I had read, for screenwriters to keep much of the movie that played in their heads as they typed off the page. Leave just a basic plot structure in its place.

I think this all makes sense from an ethical and an intentional point of view[3]. If we were *intending* to represent our story top-to-bottom/bottom-to-top we wouldn't convey it in a form that virtually no one would consume for aesthetic and/or entertainment value *per se*. Neither would we write our story in a form requiring dozens and dozens of film workers to bring to a state where people *would* consume it for such value. Since screenwriters are choosing the path where dozens must function in collaboration to complete the work, screenwriters *ought* also be receptive to such collaboration and grant all due autonomy to co-creators. Screenwriters ought leave a sufficient amount of the audio/visuals to others, therefore.

The three golden rules that follow from the aforementioned courtesy are thus:

- Write in present tense,
- Write phenomenologically, and/or
- Write abstractly.

Leave the filling-in of the cinematic gaps to the director (possibly you the writer if you're lucky), the cinematographer (likely not you), the actors, etc. Leave your action set pieces to the choreographers and stunt coordinators too if you're including action set pieces.

---

3. The artistic point of view is a different beast altogether...

Why we write in *present tense* is obvious - with much better-utilized ink spilled on the subject by much better writers - so here's *why* in the briefest of briefs: movies happen in *the now*. Even period pieces and flashbacks are presented in *the now* of the intended point in time. To put it clunkilly, script action in flashback is elliptical for,

[it is currently the case that, at point X in the past, it is currently the case that,] the Titanic sinks ... Ilsa stands Rick up at the train station ... Vito Andolini arrives at Ellis island ... etc.

How would we represent on screen *at present* what is described as having happened in the past? It's impossible. If *the couple danced to the rhythm of the waltz* and we're seeing this on screen currently, what we're actually seeing is *the couple dance to the rhythm of the waltz.*

We *can* represent at present what is described as having happened in the past in a novel, however. Just switch the narration from present tense to past. Or, if you're already writing in past tense, keep the tense but timestamp the flashback narration to the relevant moment in the past either explicitly or through implication (ie. either *tell*, or *show*, respectively)[4].

Note that we can read it as *represented* this way but our theatre of the mind won't *present* it to us this way. Like the audio/visual depictions of cinema, this is impossible as the 'theater' of the mind is also 'in the now'.

A movie's a time machine. A novel's a history lesson.

---

[4]. I won't comment on the *necessity/lack-of-necessity* of the principle, 'show, don't tell' here.

PART II: SOME STRAIGHTFORWARD ADVICE

We write screenplays *phenomenologically* for reasons nearly as obvious: a film cannot depict the subjectivity of characters nor the causality/entailment of events, only the audio/visual *phenomena* the camera picks up[5]. As an exercise, try to depict the following two pieces of action purely aurally and visually:

> She burst through the door in a state of lament, images of the job interview flashing across her mind's eye: her stammering, her freezing up, her snobbish criticism of what would turn out to be office art selected by the CEO's wife...

and,

> The second he touched the handle, the intense heat *made* him recoil.

With the former example, lamentation is perhaps able to be depicted behavioristically, but everything else would require a change of scene: a flashback perhaps or the character unconvincingly muttering descriptions of the failed interview to herself. You could add some sort of thought bubble effect, *ala* a cartoon, and push in on it as it displays a picture-in-picture-style representation of the character's thoughts... But... Talk about clunky...

For the latter piece of action on screen, the causal aspect

---

5. And the audio equipment and the optical effects equipment and the digital effects equipment and...

is strictly implied and could be more economically written as follows:

> The second he touched the handle, he recoiled.

What would be lost in the depiction by removing *the intense heat made him...*?

For the economy and believability of it, screenwriters describe only qualities of people, places, and things that can be seen or heard. That is, they write phenomenologically.

Lastly, we write abstractly as any more-detailed representation of a concept is not guaranteed - should we be lucky enough to see a screenplay produced - to be retained by the director or anyone else deciding what ends up on screen. Take Quinten Tarantino's iconic (and elaborate) dance scene in *Pulp Fiction*. For all it's unique choreography, the 123 page version of Tarantino and Roger Avary's script described the scene thus:

 Mia and Vincent dance to Chuck Berry's "You Never Can Tell". They make hand movements as they dance[6].

Shooting scripts are much more elaborate in description, but for the *sell the movie* draft we get no indication of what the dance will look like save for it involving hand movements. Here we are simply given the concept of *dance*

---

6. The *Pulp Fiction* script was accessed from the Internet Movie Script Database.

PART II: SOME STRAIGHTFORWARD ADVICE

and the concept of *hand movements*, no specifics about what type of dance or what it will look like on screen. Although a dance with hand movements is able to be represented aurally/visually, the specifics are left to the film workers to determine[7]. We are only given the concepts.

As mentioned, *Interventionism* and *Bedside Manner* were overwritten as screenplays. However, they were woefully underwritten (and written in the wrong way) for novels. All the excess elaboration applied in certain set pieces didn't help me when it came to recovering the unstated logic, subtext, and other connective tissue left offscreen[8], *i.e.* elements I needed for the big picture. Because I wrote those screenplays before the novels, both phenomenologically and/or abstractly too, and I waited near a year before adapting them to novels, I lost the movie. I couldn't remember the movie that was playing in my head when I wrote it, nor could the bare-bones script jog that memory.

Now, if I had written the novel first, I would have had *carte blanche* to include all the detail I wanted (at least in earlier drafts) and the movie in my head would be the movie I wanted my readers to have in their heads[9]. That movie, that fodder for theatre of the mind, would have been retained in the novel all those months later, hence recoverable for the screenplay.

If you're anything like me, avoiding this eventuality

---

7. In this case, Tarantino himself, as he was already on board as director, but this still didn't save him from having to write a more streamlined version of his and Avary's script.
8. But perfectly fine to include in a book (in the right dose and manner....).
9. My ability to articulate my ideas notwithstanding...

alone is sufficient justification for writing the novel first. That said, here's another justification...

THE NOVEL REIFIES THE STORY IN ALL ITS DETAIL

As said, my screenplays were *blooooooaaaaaattttted*. If 90 to 120 pages is the 'acceptable' range, and 100 to 110 pages is the sweet spot, 160+ pages is in the *I'm not even trying to play the Hollywood game and will never find work* zone.

The reason for the bloat was fairly straightforward: despite knowing the three rules of the screenwriter's courtesy, I couldn't suppress that nagging desire to put 'my vision' on the page. From the keyboard I was choreographing the dance and fight scenes, doing ballistics for the shootouts, coordinating stunts for vehicle crashes, doing the cinematography, even including music for the soundtrack. I easily added an hour of screen time to my movie because it was *my* movie (which it wasn't).

Why do I say I added time to the movie instead of just pages to the script? Read the first few pages of any book on screenwriting and you'll hear about the ratio,

1 page of script to 1 minute of screen time,

Viz. filming one page of your script will result in one minute of movie on the screen.

Now, you could argue that this ratio is inexact and silly and it would be an easy argument to make. Consider that a page of dialogue delivered by two fast talking grifters would never take up more than a minute of screen time where a wall of a page of action detailing a car chase, in broad beats, would certainly take many.

PART II: SOME STRAIGHTFORWARD ADVICE

So why the persistence of the principle? I suspect the ratio is more an attempt at finding justification in hind-sight for a writing requirement that works enough of the time. Sometimes we just figure out what works most effectively and efficiently via the bottom up, through trial and error, but then think to ourselves *there must have been some reason/design to this*. There isn't I'd bet, but just like you can set your watch to the fact that a budding screenwriter wants his whole vision on the page, you can also set your watch to the fact that an executive wants credit for having planned an accidental outcome[10]. Regardless, the *1-page:1-minute* standard is believed to serve more of a use than less so will be around until it isn't.

I defied that standard of course, where I'm sure I wouldn't have if I had written the novel first. I could have rested easy knowing all the punches, kicks, helicopter explosions, reverse fleckerls, and on... were on the page of a finished product available for consumption should the script not sell (which it wouldn't[11]).

Let the love interests *duke it out* and the hero and villain *waltz* and let the film workers make it work. I've already told *my* story over there anyway...

TEARING A NOVEL DOWN TO A SCREENPLAY IS EASIER THAN BUILDING A SCREENPLAY UP TO A NOVEL.

Stupidly, I adapted my scripts by copying and pasting the text from Final Draft to Word. I then standardized all the

---

10. I don't actually know what executives want. I don't work in their industry.
11. To film *Interventionism* would easily cost multiple hundreds of millions.

text margins to 2.5cm and added quotation marks and the appropriate indentations to the dialogue. This left a pretty horrible novel. It read like the narrator was a robot without any understanding that human beings have minds with thoughts, beliefs, desires and the like - as well as imagination. There was no subjectivity present just description of phenomena. Further, a bloated script at 160 pages condenses to less than 120 pages in manuscript format. *Ah man! You mean I gotta write 130 more pages? At least?*

And man, I was so tempted to leave it at 120 pages of robot tale[12]... Again, I had lost the movie at this point, so if I couldn't even pad out and elaborate on the things seen and heard, how could I get back into my characters' heads and remember what they were thinking any given scene? I couldn't, so I had to make it up as I went along and hope the subjectivity would remain consistent with the plot points betrayed by the action, behaviour, and dialogue.

Of course, if I had written the novel first, thought in the novel could have been scripted (lazily) to become dialogue or, with a bit more effort, behaviouristic. Never forget, actors have an amazing ability to betray thoughts, feelings, and attitudes in their facial expressions, body language, and tone of voice. A *wistful look* at a photo of a loved one, or a *lascivious look* from one spouse to a non-spouse - in the presence of the other spouse[13] - may not be worth a thousand words, but those looks in the right context will make a point far better than flat description in a novel or dialogue in a script. In fact, adapting a novel to a script may betray passages in the former where a description of action or behaviour would *show* your story to the reader in a far more

---

12. I barely managed to do any better with the final novels, and it shows!
13. Billy Wilder's maneuver I believe...

interesting manner than the inner monologue of a character (or an omniscient narrator) could *tell* it.

Near invariably, a novel contains a script where a script doesn't contain a novel. This is similar to how a house with all it's decor and fixtures contains a frame where the frame doesn't contain the house. It would be much easier to tear a house down to its frame - to build back up again - knowing you can keep any of the fixtures, decor, and appliances you please, as opposed to trying to build from a featureless frame after you've lost your blueprint.

Play architect, contractor, and decorator up front.

I'd have saved myself a lot of time if I were doing a tear-down as opposed to a rebuild, and, if you're like me, you will too.

CONCLUSION

The end.

BATCH PUBLISHING AND AVOIDING THE SOPHOMORE CURSE (AN EXPERIMENT)

YOU CAN'T HAVE A FAILED SECOND WORK IF YOU DON'T HAVE A SECOND WORK.

In what follows I will detail a semi-well-known problem in the world of content creation: *the sophomore curse* (or, *the curse*). I will focus on the curse in filmmaking in particular. Although a feature of genre fiction writing and comics/graphic novel writing, the curse is much easier to pick out in the world of cinema due the costs, complexity, and labor-intensiveness of film production (more on why this matters shortly).

Next, I will detail a release model for fictional content that denies the curse (but a model with potential problems of its own), laying the groundwork for a chronicling of the effectiveness of my use of this model (implemented the day of this piece's initial publication: December 31, 2023).

But first...

PART II: SOME STRAIGHTFORWARD ADVICE

WHAT'S THE SOPHOMORE CURSE?

The sophomore curse - not to be confused with *the sophomore slump* or *the sophomore jinx,* where a second-year university student fails to achieve the same motivation and success she achieved in her first year - is a phenomenon, experienced by some artists, marked by...

> *The sudden diminishment of reputation, as well as marketability of the artist's work, subsequent to the release of a second work, deemed less successful than the first.*[1]

Note that the concept seems similar to that of *one hit wonder*. However, the curse is conceptually dissimilar in at least one important way: an artist considered a one hit wonder need not have his best work be his first, whereas the victim of the sophomore curse *does* require that his best work be his first. Logically, you could say, a victim of the curse is a one hit wonder, but a one hit wonder isn't necessarily a victim of the curse.

As stated in the section above, the curse is more prominent among filmmakers. The costs and complexity involved in filmmaking determine the risk/reward ratio of production so much greater, hence, the decision to not take a chance on a fledgling filmmaker so much more likely. Cases of the

---

1. This is a more generalized definition of the curse, with the more specific variant referring to filmmaking exclusively. I was first introduced to (the concept I've decided to call for the purposes of differentiation) *the sophomore curse* by film producer Lawrence Bender. He discusses the curse in the documentary, *Quentin Tarantino: 20 Years of Filmmaking*. Oddly enough, he used the term 'the sophomore jinx' but articulated the concept used in this article.

sophomore curse in filmmaking are more easily identifiable and definable, therefore, due their greater frequency and severity.

Despite the greater severity of the curse in filmmaking, the degree of diminishment of reputation and marketability differs case by case. Filmmakers do not necessarily fall off a cliff of obscurity when subject to the curse, never to work again. Instead, some just fail to achieve a greater (or even the same) amount of success as they did with their first work.

For some, the diminishment is marked but not career-killing. Kevin Smith, for example, had several good films after the disappointing-by-Hollywood-standards *Mallrats*, but *Chasing Amy* and *Dogma* never received the same attention *Mallrats* did, nor the proportional increase in production value that *Mallrats* received relative to *Clerks*. Richard Kelly on the other hand - and end of the curse spectrum - has only directed one other feature after following up on *Donnie Darko* with the poorly-received *Southland Tales*.

What's the cause of the curse? The predominating hypothesis (not proven theory, mind you!) suggests that everyone from corporate executives who might buy and sell the artist's works, to representatives of the artist, to potential consumers of the artist's subsequent works, have written the artist off as someone who only had one good idea, knocked that one out of the park, then had nothing left in the tank[2]. Those previously interested in the artist's work now believe he's got nothing of quality left to produce, or so says the hypothesis.

This may provide the correct explanation, but if so, it's based on a false picture of how creative types actually create

---

2. Like how I now have nothing left in my metaphor tank...

(not to mention market their works). I've never heard of a single artist who's ever *penned, inked, pencilled, painted, sculpted, strummed, tooted, bowed, shot, danced,* or *sang* (or more) a single first work and then did nothing until that work was issued to the public for their consumption[3]. (Let's focus on writers for a bit). Near all anecdotes of famous writers discussing the lead-up to the release of their first work tell this story:

Many works were submitted to agents, editors, publishers, producers, etc. where - after the barrier of form-letter rejections was broken down and someone finally agreed to look at the content - at least two things happened:

1. The person solicited asked, *what else ya got?*
2. (If the person solicited wanted to do business...) the person solicited shared those additional materials with other people in the industry.

These two outcomes suggest the hypothesis not just one implying mass irrationalism, but one that's straightforwardly false. First-time writers rarely ever possess just a single work of promise, and even more rarely are the people who help them publish or produce their works unaware of this. Since industry representatives and decision-makers know our hypothetical writer has multiple works of quality, it would be contradictory to believe the writer only had one work of quality in the hopper - prior to the sophomore failure - and the failed sophomore effort proves this. The

---

3. Although there are almost certainly exceptions to this, these exceptions are rarities.

hypothesis, if true, means the majority of industry insiders are dishonest and/or stupid. This is unlikely[4].

So, why would multiple industries (and these industries' consumers) near-invariably cut an artist loose after one failed work...

But not if it's the first...
Not if it's the third...
Not if it comes at any point after the third...
But *only* if it's the second?
Honestly? Who knows... But they do.

ASIDE: THE SECONDARY SOPHOMORE CURSE FOR CREATORS OF SERIES.

For creators of content that has a reified[5] 'first' of a series (e.g. the first issue of a comic/magazine, the first chapters of a serialized novel, the first time a notable writer contributed to a publication, etc.) there's a secondary curse. The second is marked by:

> *The sudden diminishment of marketability of the creator's works, subsequent to the release of a second issue/sequel of a reified series/edition, of less/more/same degree of quality as the first.*

The explanation for this variant is much more straightforward (and almost certainly true): when buyers of serial publications see a '# 1' on a comic, magazine, etc. they buy

---

4. Make the obvious jokes, but this is false on matters of fact.
5. The *reified* constraint may no longer be necessary as, with the growing popularity of NFTs, digital 'firsts' can have singular owners of the *type* of the *token* digitizations, hence collectibility and investment potential.

multiple copies for investment/collector purposes. A '# 2' just doesn't have the same effect.

The secondary curse means 2x the potential for undue and unfairly/irrationally imposed obscurity, right? Interestingly, this secondary curse, should it be anticipated by creators, is no curse at all. Fewer sales of a second work do not necessarily create the impression of exhausted talent in those interested in consuming the series for its creative merits *per se*. They care about quality not sales.

No drop in quality of the second work, no curse. In fact, the secondary 'curse' can be downright desirable. Publishers who've established popularity of a particular property produced as a series often create multiple, limited runs, of additional series of that property to bank on greater numbers of sales of '# 1's on shelves[6].

So, nothing to worry about with the secondary curse, then? Unfortunately, for creators just starting out, a lack of awareness of the secondary curse means having to contend with the shock of a tremendous drop in sales (and assumed popularity). Where there's this lack of understanding, there's still the curse because, where there's this lack of understanding, there's a potentially huge blow to the creator's motivation. In this case, the *secondary sophomore curse* actually becomes the *sophomore jinx*!

OVERCOMING THE CURSE WITH BATCH PUBLICATION

The plan for overcoming the sophomore curse is simple: have no sophomore work. I released two novels on the same

---

6. Todd McFarlane discusses this phenomenon in the world of comics here https://www.youtube.com/watch?v=hoMq3tGaT5U&t=1991s

day I originally published this chapter as an article, and, with each subsequent publication, I intended there to be multiple works published concurrently[7]. If one work is weaker than the other, call that work the *first* and consider the other an improvement. If they're equally bad, then that's one hell of an unlikelihood and one hell of a precision metric you have there! Can I borrow it?

Of course, there are marketing concerns with this model. I don't know what they are, but there are concerns (*known unknowns*, as they say). After all, multiple unique properties of fiction released simultaneously from the same creator are exceptionally rare (for good reason?). Unknown marketing issues notwithstanding, with this model - *this* experiment - I intend to test the hypothesis: *the sophomore curse can be avoided with batch publication at minimal to no impairment of success otherwise.* If marketing issues become apparent in this process, and I can't find any feasible means of resolving them, then that is evidence of the hypothesis' failure and the experiment is still of use.

As far as experimental controls go, I have none. Since I'm not going to publish multiple collections of works according to the above model under multiple pen names (and then do the same using the traditional model), I only get one kick at the can of self-publishing for the first time. I only get one application of one model for the first time, therefore.

The only process for gathering evidence that my outcome would have been different *all things equal BUT an application of the batch publishing model* would be to analyze cases that are sufficiently close to being *all things equal* to my method, then compare these cases' outcomes to the

---

7. Pulled this off up to my fifth publication.

outcomes of cases that are *all things equal* to my method, minus the batch publishing. The problem here is, the batch publishing model is exceptionally rare, so the chances of *all things equal* cases existing among such a small subset of publication types are virtually none.

Regardless, I'll barrel on. I'll start by meeting the first condition necessary for my hypothesis to be tested: *having at least one of my first two publications be wildly successful*[8].

I'll let you know how it goes.

THE RESULT (AS OF AUGUST 10, 2025)

It went badly[9].

---

8. Shouldn't be a problem...

9. As in, it *was* a problem. But that doesn't falsify my claim. This only means there's insufficient evidence for proof. So try out the batch publishing method if you've got the popularity to pull it off.

SOME SINGLE STORY-THREAD NOVELS ARE LIKE MOVIES, SOME ARE LIKE CABLE TV SEASONS...

TOO SHORT AND STRAIGHTFORWARD? TOO MEANDERING AND LONG-WINDED? DEPENDS...

Lately I've been trying to write something more discursive and elaborate. By *discursive* and *elaborate* I mean: meandering and long-winded. You know, the way those novelists who tell a simple self-contained story manage to do and in a way that requires *at least* 350 pages (and doesn't seem meandering at all)? But I feel like I'm going to fail at this.

I busted my ass to get one of my past novels to 250 pages. I included flashbacks, monologues, inner-monologues, even on-the-nose symbolism about dogs burying bones and not-so-on-the-nose symbolism about defiant trees *for crying out loud!* It was torture. By page 160 I was spent. By page 160 of any book, I'm spent. Don't get me wrong, tell me to write something in a 90-page screenplay and I'll get to 220 pages in a yawn[1]. But with a book, I'm done. I've told a story with a

---

1. Too bad nobody's ever told me this with their money!

PART II: SOME STRAIGHTFORWARD ADVICE

beginning, middle, and end, with some extra bells and whistles thrown in, and there's nothing else left to say.

Why?

Because I write novels like movies. That's what I see in my head. That's how I write about the writing process too. That's how a lot of people write about the writing process (and reading!). *Theater of the mind* we all say, but we don't mean some dialogue-heavy proscenium set play. We mean elaborate, grand, broad in geographical scope, often bombastic, intentionalistic audio-visual epicry. My books are movies. They got three acts. They're predictable that way. And, I like 'em that way. And yet, some of the best novels, that tell a single story with minimal subplots, stretch on forever and are quite well received[2]...

Why?

Because these writers write novels like 8 to 10-episode seasons of cable television shows? I *ask* this because I can't read their minds. But, the explanation: *these writers see one of several individuated 5 act vignettes in their heads, where a single story arc occurs across these vignettes with plenty of space to explore backstory, character, and events with greater profundity*, is a pretty damn consistent explanation if I do do so my doof...

I finally read *The Shining* this year and, without going too far down the path of critique, I was struck by how simple the story was despite the nearly 700 pages. How'd Stephen King cover that much ground with just a story about a family with special gifts in a hotel with malevolent powers? How? With plenty of backstory, digression, elaboration on characters, and constant windows into everybody's minds. You can fill a lot of space if you give the same

---

2. And, for some petty reason, I want in that club?

amount of time to a character's thoughts, feelings, and attitudes as you do that character's words and deeds.

These maneuvers fill up the page, but, in the case of writers like King, what makes them *work*? Why are his stories engaging to readers (and not boring like mine[3])? I think it's the fact that, as mentioned, the books of King and others can be broken down into vignettes. In *The Shining* we have an entire chapter devoted to Jack, the protagonist, reading a scrapbook about the titular hotel, *The Shining Hotel*. That's not true. The hotel's name is *The Overlook*: the titular character of *Dr. Sleep*. Now, as I said, a chapter of *The Shining* deals entirely with Jack reading a scrapbook (scrapbook entries included verbatim), and it's not boring.

Why's this not boring? I can conjecture a few reasons. First, King does a good job piquing readers' interests in the mysteries of The Overlook. Awful things have happened there and nobody knows why. Two people with extrasensory perception have bad feelings about the place but can't exactly explain why. The place has an ominous air to it, appears to have a weird hold on certain people, and we all want to know why. King's also developed his protagonist sufficiently well enough that we know he's a complex man[4] - has made mistakes but is redeeming himself - yet there's a clear vulnerability and potential for a world of different types of relapses. We're interested, therefore, in The Overlook *per se*, Jack *per se*, and how the two relate to each other. Jack's inner monologuing along to his and our reading of the scrapbook is the right framing for this chapter.

Notice though, that the chapter itself is decidedly

---

3. That's not fair. I don't have enough readers to know if my stuff is generally boring... or boring to anyone! (Feedback is always welcome...)
4. Jack Torrence, not King.

PART II: SOME STRAIGHTFORWARD ADVICE

similar to so many television season episodes of shows as varied as The Sopranos, Firefly, Better Call Saul, and many more, where we are given a series of flashbacks themed around an inorganic non-intentional character[5], in order to better understand that character. I'm thinking of episodes of The Sopranos where we see the evolution of Tony's Jersey neighbourhood throughout his childhood. That episode of Firefly where we learn about the origin of Serenity and its crew. Those episodes of Breaking Bad and Better Call Saul where we learn of the origins of the El Pollos Hermanos complex of chicken restaurants and meth labs. If The Shining were a TV season, this could be a flashback episode. All this said, the chapter works because the passages, like the flashbacks of the aforementioned TV episodes, tell a story in themselves.

So, do writers like King model their single story-thread novel structures after television seasons?

Maybe they do, maybe they don't, but probably they don't (maybe they do non-consciously?). As I understand it, King's writing process is largely improvisational. He sits down at the typewriter and just writes what comes to mind and lets those thoughts-now-on-the-page determine where to go next, narratively. He's what some people who give writing advice call a 'pantser', as in, he writes by the *seat of his pants* (as opposed to writers who pre-plan and outline).

---

5. Yeah, I think inorganic non-intentional objects can be characters. I almost think a sufficient condition for any object to be a character is that audiences *care* about it like they would something with personhood (Oh no! The Starship Enterprise Exploded! ... Oh Yeah! The Death Star exploded! ... Oh boy! Rosebud exploded! ...). If not sufficient, then add the fact that certain non-personal inorganic objects have *character* themselves (Marcellus Wallace's briefcase is a real charmer...), or derived intentionality (Marcellus Wallace's briefcase is real manipulative). *Care* and *character* are sufficient for *character*, or am I wrong?

Alright, unless *length*-writers come forward to tell us that *indeed, they picture not a movie in their heads as they write but a series of interconnected episodes of something like a TV show*, we can't really assume that's a part of their method. But why not use this technique when looking to broaden your fiction writing chops? If you never find yourself at a loss for how to broach a new style, start a work according to that style, and/or maintain it, then *forget-you* lucky! But, if you do feel like a strategy would help, try the TV/Movie model.

Want a quicker read for your audience, model your story after a movie (keeping in mind you can add whatever *accoutrement* you want if you get desperate). Want to give them a world and some people to spend a hell of a lot more time with, model your novel after an eight-episode season of television.

How do you do these things exactly? Watch a lot of movies and TV and then take notes.

GETTIN' PRECIOUS

GOING FROM SILLY IDEAS TO SILLY IDEAS THAT MATTER TOO MUCH TO NOT BE PERFECT (AND BACK AGAIN...)

INTRODUCTION

I was about to start this article with the opening clause: *As an erstwhile writer.* Then I looked up the word 'erstwhile' and it turns out, though still fancy, *erstwhile* meant *former* all along!

I'm not a former writer. I'm doing it now!

THE REST OF THE ARTICLE

As a writer writing right now, I have one rule:

Any time I'm reading, watching, reading, listening, but ninety-nine percent of the time not reading anything but instead listening to an audiobook[1] and I come up with a criticism or interpretation of the work I'm consuming, where that criticism or interpretation would substantially change the story if applied, I have to write that story

---

1. **Youtube video giving a synopsis of the book.*

myself. Or, at the very least, write its premise onto my little digital notepad.

'Why didn't that character that did that stupid thing do the smart thing instead?' I might ask as I watch an episode of *Simon & Simon*...

Well, regardless of the answer to my question, the exploits of that 'character doing that smart thing' is a story in itself. And, since those exploits are literally the opposite of what just happened in the story I'm currently immersed in, it's a new story so you can't sue me if I tell it. Of course, by *that's a story*[2] I really mean *that's a premise*. The premise will be what is opposite and so unique (but ya still gotta change everything else that's the same).

Case in point, at some *point* across my numerous viewings of *The Terminator*, I was struck by the imprudence of the Reese character in how he protected Sarah Connor:

If Reese knew all along where Sarah lived[3] and The Terminator didn't, why didn't Reese just snatch her up, drive her to safety (before Terminator could get anywhere near her), then convince her of her importance in the future *instead* of watching her for a day and a half only to just let The Terminator get right up beside her, shoot her in the hair, traumatize her, and only after that: snatch her up, try to drive her to safety, then convince her of her importance in the future?[4]

Why indeed? I don't know. But I do know two other

---

2. *When the sun's up your butt like some old Pizza Hut that's a storé!*
3. He sat in her parking garage in the dark watching her get on her motor scooter and ride after all...
4. Let's assume here we're judging the movie for internal logic alone and can't just fall back on the meta-justification: *because then the movie couldn't happen...*

PART II: SOME STRAIGHTFORWARD ADVICE

things: first, I had a unique premise on my hands here[5] and second, to realize it I'd have to get rid of all the robots and time machines and character names and essential character attributes... Basically everything. Even then the premise was not likely to be original enough or have legs. But a new premise is valuable nonetheless and ought be saved for posterity.

So, any time you catch yourself thinking:

- *I don't think the good guys are so good, the bad guys are kinda better...*

That's a story.

- *This zombie bromance biopic plays more like a coming of age period rockumentary...*

That's a story, boy.

- *Nobody would do business with a hitman who takes money from the people he's about to kill to kill the guys who hired him to kill the people he's about to kill thereby leaving everyone involved killed, even the hitman because he's established himself as a killer who will kill anyone and therefore can't be trusted...*

Story! Story! Story! Story! That's a story!
*Some of the above examples are based on actual critiques

---

5. I.e. *a man kidnaps a woman in order that he prepare her for her essential role in a future event of monumental importance, slowly wearing her down, but is he on the level, or just crazy...*

(Still too Terminatory for my tastes...)

and some are just silly nonsense (and one of the real ones is based on 'The Good The Bad and The Ugly').

How about this one:

- *There's no way the aliens in 'They Live' would waste all their resources coming to earth to steal what little resources there were of ours. They'd need n-times more resources just to travel to Earth than they'd ever pilfer.*

I actually wrote an article motivating this contention. It's incredibly convincing. You'll hate it. Check it out![6]

I then decided to put my money where my mouth was and write a book based on this newly derived premise involving benevolent travelers who everyone treated as villainous but who were in fact benevolent (told you so), where it's the xenophobic humans who were the bad guys. It's not as trite as it sounds. Check it out.[7]

But, how seriously should you take these quasi-derivative premises should you undertake to put any one to page? You may be thinking, *I don't know but why not just wing it? Maybe it'll be fun and frivolous, maybe it'll be epic.* Or you might be thinking, *make it frivolous (coming up with the idea certainly was).* Or even, *make it your magnum opus, every work has its influences.*

I don't know the correct answer to the above question but I do have a story of a story for you: a case of coming up with a premise then winging it. My story might just be illuminating (or, at the very least, self-indulgent).

---

6. https://medium.com/@djwinters101/really-the-ghouls-in-they-live-are-the-good-guys-c8e6c1a0e677
7. https://books2read.com/u/3Gg5Jr

PART II: SOME STRAIGHTFORWARD ADVICE

I wrote a book that went from being a frivolous lark, to a precious mess-cious, to something I had to tone right the heck down, to a final draft that turned out to be something I'm actually kinda proud of. It all started with one of those observations... The observation was this:

- *Ya know what, 'The Exorcist' totally plays out like a western in structure, especially throughout the third act. You've got a US Marshal running a miscreant out of a western town where the marshal's your exorcist and the Miscreant's your demon. You've got the Sheriff as the assisting priest. The mayor as the mom. And the wild west town itself as the child possessed. The old marshal rides into town and with the help of the mayor and the sheriff runs the bad guy out. It all fits.*

What a silly idea to hang a 400 page novel on... But that's the idea I committed to realizing and the 400 page novel is what resulted. The story was called *The Taking of Shale City*.[8]

It started out as a writing project where the hardest part would be not infringing on copyrighted material. I had all my analogues to the original Exorcist—film or novel, take you pick—and not just the characters but the iconic shots, scenes, and set pieces. All I intended to do was lay these analogues out in manuscript form, beat for beat, and not break any of those aforementioned laws (I never thought it would come to fruition anyway). But then...

Then the metastasis...

What started out as a fun (and maybe a little audacious)

---

8. https://books2read.com/u/mK5dBP

parody turned into the most precious (and pretentious) mess you've ever seen. A simple story about lawmen running bad men outta town became an ode to fatherhood, a meditation on our moral sentiments and their role in our moral actions, a history of my Ukrainian ancestors' persecution, folk economics that would make Milton Friedman proud (to have never known me), a strangely prescient commentary on tariffs, homages to everything from *Night of the Living Dead* to *Big Trouble in Little China*, and the chasing of a dream from beyond the grave! And redemption! And... AND!... Farming.

It was also written in vernacular throughout the first few drafts[9]. It was exactly what you'd expect for a work written in vernacular. Actually, I bet it wasn't. I bet it was *worse* than you'd expect. It was a single-handed, one-fell-swoop substantiation of Elmore Leonard's rule number 7 for fiction writers: *use regional dialect and patois sparingly*. I used a lot of *ain't*s and *not neither*s and *reck'n*s. Pretty bad if I do say so myself. There was also a liberal use of the prime symbol (') in place of the letter 'G', ala *figurin'*, *runnin'*, *lumberin'*, etc.

Alright, so I ditched the vernacular and paté (?) the best I could but I couldn't completely but I did my best and I was relieved. But then I got a little scared of all the damn commas (punctuation in general). But then I got the bright Idea to get rid of all the punctuation like I was Cormac McCarthy or something. I did a *search and replace* and replaced everything but the periods with nothing. Then I got scared of all them unconstrained linguistic elements and chickened out. I put back the quotation marks and added a comma here and there.

---

9. Though I like to call it *Barn-acular* because the story involves horses and agriculture and I fancy myself too clever by half...

Did I mention that I wrote and published the thing in less than four months? Well I did. That's kinda my model for this whole enterprise: quick and dirty genre fiction that's fun with the odd bit of upmarket pomposity thrown in. It took me four months and that's twice as long as these things usually take me and that was because of all the goddamn preciousness. The thing had to be authentic, but read fluently. The commas were distracting but no commas at all made it look plain weird. Would people get the subtext? Would people hate the prose I'd added to make explicit the subtext I wanted people to 'get' that wasn't subtext at all anymore all things considered? What if nobody reads this? What if anybody reads this? What if *everybody* reads this? Will they get the *Ghostbusters* reference?[10]

So I pared things down then added more, pared then added. I don't know how to write but I know how to feel and so I just kept repeating this add/remove dialectical manoeuvre[11] until reading the thing didn't *feel* so bad.

Then I let it sit.

Apropos of everything, it's worth mentioning that many famous and successful writers hate rereading what they've written and I'm not one of them because I'm neither famous nor successful. But take away their fame and success and I am one of them. I'm also a glutton for punishment. I can't help but crack open any ebook version of any of my stuff in the hopes I'll convince myself things ain't so bad.

Thing's are always so bad.

There's always something to make me wanna unpublish all over myself. But, going into this knowing my sucking's not a matter of *does-or-does-not* but *does-to-what-degree* really

---

10. Not a joke.
11. I don't write it 'maneuver' I write it *maneuvray*!

helped add a layer of *why-even-bother* to the *this-is-going-to-hurt-so-bad*. (So, phew?)

Ok writer, how many times will you be struck by the urge to baff between those digital pages of the passages you're rereading?

Well, ya know what, the book cringed me out a great many times but nowhere near as many as my other books had. Could have been a lot worse. Lettin' it get so precious was torturous but it was a learning lesson: when you get so worked up about leaving your best work on the page you end up leaving *all* your work on the page and so, *a fortiori*, your best stuff's gotta be in there somewhere. You just gotta find it...

(And to think, I started this whole writing endeavor fearful of getting sued for ripping off old horror movies. Bet I would have gotten a lot more exposure if I'd done it that way...)

CONCLUSION

Those last couple paragraphs up there are a way of ending this meandering account that's sufficiently 'ending-sounding' I reckon.

A NON-EXHAUSTIVE, NON-THREATENING, (NON-PROFESSIONAL) LIST OF WAYS RECLUSIVE WRITERS CAN POLISH THEIR WORK AND STAY MOTIVATED

IF YOU LIKE PINA COLADAS, READING ABOUT OTHERS' SHAME... SET THE PHONE TO AIRPLANE MODE, AND WE'LL MAKE OUR ⌥ ESC

INTRODUCTION

As I said in the preface, extroverts rule the world... Oh well.

What do you want? They have strength in solidarity. Introverts, I hate to break the tautology to you, do not. Can't very well *band together* to create an awareness of a world insufficiently accommodating to people who have no desire, motivation, obligation (or even capacity) to *band together*. It would be like a pacifist demanding peace by letter bomb (write your demands on the *outside* of the envelope I guess...).

Us introverts are poorly understood you see. By definition, very few people are ever made privy to our thoughts and feelings. Also, you can't observe us in the wild. Introversion isn't just poorly understood (and, by extension, excellently under-appreciated). Introversion is treated as downright *unhealthy*... Like an affliction.

Consider this: the average person tells someone he's outgoing and desires maximal social interaction and he'll likely get an *oh yeah?* then crickets. But try this on for size introverts, if you dare... Tell someone you're reclusive and prefer your solitude and what will you get? If you're anything like me, you'll get one of these: *oh, I used to be like you, you'll get over it, just put yourself out there...*

Like you've just told a spinach farmer you're iron deficient...

Of course what you'll never hear is *that's great! The world needs people like you! Since you're less concerned with what most people think, you take more chances creatively, and are more likely to innovate! Keep doing what you're doing and if there's anything I can do to NOT help, feel free to NOT let me know!* (Never gonna happen...).

Introversion is the 21st century's 1930s left-handedness.

Why though? Introverts are as necessary to a flourishing society as extroverts are. Since we're most content to live in our own heads, and *alienation without demonetization* is all we could ever hope for, introverts innovate more (on average). Since extroverts are most content running their ideas by others and hearing the ideas of others, their creative output is more polished and refined (on average). Conversely, due the conflicting nature of these traits, introverts aren't as polished and extroverts aren't as innovative. However, regardless of the symbiotic relationship between introverts and extroverts, and the necessity of both groups, the world just doesn't value what the introvert has to offer the same way it values what the extrovert does.

PART II: SOME STRAIGHTFORWARD ADVICE

POLISHING AND COPING ALL BY YOURSELF

Not even writing, a decidedly solitary and introspective activity, can escape this extrovert-*centric* world of ours. Wanna succeed at writing? Then...

- *Network! network! network!*
- *Consult with beta readers!*
- *Take writing courses/attend writers conferences!*
- *Find a mentor!*
- *Join a writer's group!*

That's just a sampling of what you'll get if you search 'get your writing noticed', 'find inspiration', 'polish your work', 'prepare a manuscript for publishing'.

Seriously! Not all writers are introverts but it's got to be an activity that filters people like us in by the ton. If there's one occupation where introverts are overrepresented, it's writing. So why's all writing advice tailored to the most outgoing and gregarious people you've ever seen?

Again, because extroverts rule the world.

Not all extroverts of course, but it takes a certain pushyness to control an entire industry of people and it takes a healthy dose of extroversion to be successfully pushy and controlling. Maybe there are authoritarian introverts, but all they'd demand is that you leave them alone. Since no one wants to hang out with a pushy goon, the authoritarian introvert will never need to coercively wield *that* authority anyway, and you'll never know he's an authoritarian...

Paradox.

Naturally, because controlling people requires being around people, extroverts control people. Even more naturally, people in control of things tend to suit themselves first, often exclusively, hence the suiting of the extrovert in the writing industry (or any industry).

Oh well...

Look, let's be honest with ourselves introverts. We'll probably never develop a successful writing career working *solely* down on the farm. We'll eventually have to bite the bullet and breathe more than our own carbon dioxide. However, I think there are a few ways to generate publisher/producer/agent-ready written works without having to leave the house (or, at the very least, enter anyone else's).

Note that the common features of all services and relationships bullet-pointed above are: a fresh pair of eyes reading a writer's work *and* like-minded people providing each other encouragement and moral support. What follows then is a brief list of methods I've applied to approximate a 'fresh eye' and reduce excess insecurity. A brief list whose items, I'm just now coming to realize, introverts and recluses are almost certainly aware of. *Hey! Guy in the middle of a noon-day desert with no skin pigment whatsoever... Have you thought about using sun block?*

Oh well...

Here's the list anyway, in case you hit your head and need to jog your memory...

1. BEER DRAFT

It's called *the beer draft* but really any type of booze will do (just not light beer). It's also called *the* beer draft but there need not be just one. I've been known to apply this method up to an uncountable number of times each time I write something... Four maybe?

The method is this: drink enough alcohol so that you've still got your wits about you but your inhibitions are minimal. Drink yourself to the point where you're well past any regret about those four four-cheese calzones you just finished but nowhere near ready to have that one night stand (which you wouldn't have anyway since you're an unpublished JD Salinger drinking dial-a-bottle Palm Bay coolers with just your laptop for company on an Ikea chez lounge down on the farm).

The buzz will simulate the fresh pair of eyes you need to understand your work objectively. As well, the lack of insecurity and inhibition may actually allow you to enjoy the aspects of your work that are truly creative and inspired (and not be tortured over what's still a little clunky).

You'll have to maintain the right degree of buzz however, so maybe fine tune your method over a lost weekend or two.

*Alright alright. In all seriousness: *drink excessively responsibly*.

Here's another idea, try combining the beer draft with...

2. TEXT-TO-SPEECH

How the hell did I write three 'the's in a row? It's not even like any of them ran off and over to the next line!

Your beta reader would catch the four 'the's. (Surprise! Turns out there are four! One *did* run off and over to the next line). You need a beta reader but you don't have one. *You don't want one*. Problem is, you've read your manuscript so many times you're not reading your manuscript anymore. You've near-committed it to memory so now you're just reciting it to yourself in your head[1] and you're only using the pages in front of you for the odd cue to help keep your place. What's in your head is perfect but your manuscript

---

1. Not to yourself in your big toe (or my big butt).

isn't. That's why you missed the five 'the's. (Surprise again! Turns out there were five! And *none* ran off and over to the next line and out of your dreams and into your car! You're just losing your mind!).

You need a fresh pair of eyes but you don't got 'em (and you refuse to seek 'em out). This is where *text-to-speech* functionality comes in. Let your device read your work to you. Your hearing the errors out loud will make them near inescapable. If you have a Mac, simply highlight the text and hit [⌥ OPTION] and [ESC] simultaneously[2]. If you have a PC, get a Mac.

Fine... [3]

That's it. That's all there is to it. But you probably know this...

3. VIRTUAL AND PHYSICAL LENDING LIBRARIES.

Be careful with this one. There are ethical concerns (unlike the section on writing drunk). However, these are concerns that I think we can either side-step or reconcile with sufficient considerateness and generosity. Note that this method applies mostly to novel writers, especially independent novel writers.

The leaving of books, chapters, even manuscripts (if you're sufficiently trusting) in public places with a note:

Please read and enjoy. If you're up to it, please send any

---

[2]. To tweak the reader speed, voice, and other incidentals, open *Settings*, then *Accessibility*, then *Spoken Voice*.

[3]. https://support.microsoft.com/en-us/office/use-the-speak-text-to-speech-feature-to-read-text-aloud-459e7704-a76d-4fe2-ab48-189d6b83333c

feedback to the following address... Email... Leave a review on Amazon... etc.

is as old as correspondence itself. So are those take-a-book/leave-a-book *little free libraries* and similar off-brand services. Their monetization is relatively new, however. (More on that to come...).

Obviously as long as you abide by littering laws and get the requisite permissions, leaving physical samples of your work for others to read and provide feedback (should they choose to do so) is as easy as scouting public locations where it *is* permissible to do this. Not sure if you can't leave a copy of your book in one of those little free libraries? Check the library box itself for information about the caretaker or curator and reach out via email. A good rule of thumb here, for decorums sake, is to ask permission but offer to leave a brand new book or two (of local appeal) along with your work. Never hurts to ask...

But! How do we do this completely impersonally? There are online for-fee services that allow you to deposit a chapter, manuscript, even a complete copy of your book (pending an approval process) where member readers may then read your book for free, where it is customary to *at least* leave a review. It's important to note that you aren't paying anyone for reviews. You're paying for your book to be made available for free, where: no one is obligated to even read it, let-alone provide feedback. Think of it as selling your book on consignment for nothing.

To find these services the easiest way is to just Google: *get more reviews for your book*. Be careful though, you only want the free lending services. You *DO NOT* want to pay for reviews. Currently, I'm using BookSprout's services. Considering my 'entry-level' status as a writer at present, my Book-

Sprout campaign is working better than a writer like me could hope. I'll let you know how it goes when all is said and done.

Update:

Pro: Booksprout's reviewers are much more honest and thoughtful than other reviewers on other sites.

Con: the ratio of *reader-leaving-a-review to reader-NOT-leaving-a-review* is minuscule (viz. for me at least, my readers rarely left reviews).

A QUICK NOTE

The next three list items are intended to help reclusive writers manage insecurities that often arise during the writing process. However, it's important to apply these methods in the right proportion.

No writer should strive to work in a state of complete and utter confidence in the quality of her work (sorry narcissists). She shouldn't even be striving to maintain a positive and optimistic attitude throughout much of the writing process. The reason for this is simple: there's always room for improvement, where too much confidence creates the false sense that there's nothing to improve. Therefore, too much confidence increases the likelihood of a writer failing to produce her best work.

Conversely, no writer can work in a state of excessive frustration caused by feelings of inadequacy either. The intention, then, is to help the writer find a middle-ground not anaesthetize her to any and all negativity. But, the actual moderating required to find this middle-ground is up to the writer...

4. FORMAT MATCHING

This one applies mostly to film, television, and play writers (perhaps song writers too).

Although it's tempting to seek motivation in writing a stage play, screenplay, song lyrics (and more), by attending plays, watching movies, and listening to music that inspires us, it's important to remember: *these works did not originate from a single written draft of anything and are almost certainly not the product of a single creator.*

Let's focus on screen writing in the next few passages (assuming, *mutandis mutatis,* the advice also applies to other formats).

So you're gonna be the next Joe Eszterhas but you don't even have your first slug line let-alone your first draft. What do you do first? You start watching the films that are the best of the relevant genre as well as the movies you admire most? *Wrong!* You read the best scripts of the relevant genre first.

Those movies you're intending to watch are the product of,

- draft after draft after draft...
- polish upon polish upon polish...
- likely script doctoring from other writers...
    - rewrites of the doctored script from other script doctors...
        - where, after all this, the most seasoned of those writers is chosen to write the final draft that's a filtering in of all the best

ideas of all the previous drafts of all the previous writers.

And this all happens *before* the movie is made[4].

Reading your favourite line in a script affects you differently than hearing it uttered by an actor who's mastered the craft[5] acting in a movie that's meticulously put together. It's *uttered* amazingly but only *written* serviceably in order to provide options for realizing the film in a multitude of ways. The great movies are products of excessively polished scripts further polished by the collaboration of actors, cinematographers, SFX artists, editors, and so many more, all under the guidance of a competent director.

The script all of a sudden becomes so much more quaint by comparison, often a virtual promissory note. Your sub-first draft of an unfinished screenplay, by comparison, is complete and utter garbage. So, if you set the baseline of quality at that of: *the best cinema has to offer*, you'll destroy yourself. Bland textual representations of action and speech may be great for what they are: something textual. They may show great promise too. But they can't compare to the impact of a finished film (or TV episode, or song, or play...).

Intending a script to have the aesthetic and entertainment value of a finished film is like planning a housewarming party for a floor plan.

You need to hold your written work to a high standard but only the highest standard of like-works of the like-formats. But, even *these* scripts are rewrites, far from a first draft. You don't even need to have your first reification (your

---

4. Yeah, I know, crap movies are made by applying this process too. Too many cooks. But so are the *good* movies and we're assuming our hypothetical writer is taking inspiration from good movies.
5. What's a craft?

first complete iteration of your story) come close to that. That will come later. Ideally, you would set your quality standard to that of the best writers' first drafts.

Which brings us too...

5. FIRST DRAFT GROUNDING

Find a first draft a writer makes available to help ground you in the reality that: what you see as a lack of polish, complexity, innovation, etc. is actually par for the course for a budding writer. Par for the course, as even the greats wrote and rewrote, sought advice, worked in collaboration, more... Finding something even close to the earliest draft of some master's work will keep you going like one of my run-on sentences.

But such drafts are hard to find, especially for people like you and me. However, the humility of our favourite writers is often the next best thing. I'm talking about the...

6. REGALE-ITUDE OF INEPTITUDE

Read or listen to your favorite writers discuss their many many failures. They'll tell you about the times critics and industry detractors were wrong and, more importantly, about the times they were right (and how these critiques helped them become better writers).

You'll never feel better about those form rejections, ghostings, and the harsh assessments of writing contest reviewers (who you suspect didn't even read your work anyway), than you will finding out the greats experienced the exact same thing. Why this will cheer you up is obvious: there are writers out there who are way better than you at present who were treated, by industry insiders, as way worse than you at present. You're not a bad writer, you just haven't found the right readers.

Where to find these materials...

At this point in the evolution of our technologies, I think it goes without saying that written interviews, journals, autobiographies, and more abound on the internet and in book stores. It also goes without saying that audio and video interviews abound on streaming sites, as well as social media. Contemporary writers also tend to keep a blog or newsletter, made available to the public, and/or have their own youtube channels, podcasts, etc.

Choose whomever you like of course, but can I give you one bit of advice when it comes to your selecting process? Don't read William Goldman's *Adventures in the Screen Trade* if you're looking for tales of early failure and sophomore slumps and dry spells and on... *Do* read it if you want a detailed and charming window into film making and writing in general (in my opinion it's the best book on the film industry and writing I've ever read). However, when it comes to anecdotes of failures and shortcomings, what you'll get in that wonderful book is Goldman telling you things like,

> *I suppose half of the screenplays I've written have actually seen production.*[6]
>
> — WILLIAM GOLDMAN

Half! Half of his screenplays have seen production! The *average* better-than-average screenwriter will tell you he's

---

6. Goldman, William. Adventures in the Screen Trade (p. 217). Grand Central Publishing. Kindle Edition.

written something like 60 scripts in his life, 10 were sold, 3 saw production...

That makes Goldman near a thousand percent more successful than the average writer! He's a unicorn! He's also in the top five of best screen writers of all time... So, if you read Goldman and come away thinking your probability of success is a flip of a coin, for the sake of your own sanity, I hope it's a 30-sided coin...

CONCLUSION

I don't like endings. Best of luck

PART III: MURDER MYSTERY WRITING ADVICE

THE LEAST JACKASSERY-LADEN/SMARTASSERY-LADEN, SECTION OF THIS BOOK (FEEL FREE TO SKIP...)

LET EM GET AWAY WITH IT... THEN DON'T (1 MOD 1)

THE 'PERFECT CRIME' METHOD FOR CONSTRUCTING YOUR MYSTERY

PART 1, MODULO 1: THE METHOD

Note: this chapter is broken up into two parts. One part details a novel method for constructing a mystery element of a fiction story, as well as provides an application of that method. The other part provides a story treatment generated from the application. Depending on your preference, either section can be read first.

If you want a more academic exercise, i.e. you want to gain an understanding of the method first, start with this chapter. If you want to read the treatment for the treatment's sake - i.e. you want to read the mystery treatment first to experience the twists and turns for their entertainment and aesthetic value, and then see how the mystery was built, start with Part 2.

Either way, it's up to you...

INTRODUCTION

Let's say you're writing a work of fiction that includes a mystery element. Let's also say it's either a *whodunit* (*ala* Murder She Wrote) or a *howlysolvit* (*ala* Columbo). One method you might consider in crafting your mystery is sketched thus:

1. Construct the perfect crime: conceive of a scenario where the perpetrator/perpetrators pull off the crime (or something they wouldn't want to get caught attempting) without error, get away with it completely, and then live out the rest of their lives happy, healthy, and despicable.

2. After that, go back to (*around*) the beginning of this scenario and add at least one inciting complication...
    - That creates more complications...
        - That creates more complications...
            - That forces the perp[1] to attempt a resolution that allows for a return to the original plan.

3. Have at least one of these complications catch the attention of a curious party (one or more people) who start pushing back against the perp's attempts at resolution, wittingly or unwittingly,

---

[1]. Let's just assume a single *perp* from here on, but there can be as many as you like.

which ultimately leads to the perp getting found out[2].

Make the *perfect crime* as detailed as possible. List all the players in the game and their roles. Lay out the events chronologically too, beat-for-beat. As well, before adding the inciting complication, the *pushes* and the *pulls* of the antagonism, and having the curious party reveal the perp for the perp's *perpitude*, add appropriate history and character motivation for context. Lastly, the antagonism between the curious party and the perp can involve other characters (perhaps some bystanders along the way, for example).

The key to the method is a plausible push and pull between the perp and the curious party.

Now, all this *said*... I'm sketching out a method here! We master method by *doing*, not by remembering or rehearsing an algorithm. So let's actually apply this method.

A SOMEWHAT ELABORATE EXAMPLE:

Let's apply this method according to a hastily thrown-together crime scenario, full of cliches and tropes, that will nevertheless illustrate the method[3]. When I first started writing this and got to this point in the article, my television

---

2. Not necessarily caught or brought to justice, just revealed to be the perpetrator. Why not necessarily brought to justice? Forget it valued reader, it's Chinatown...

3. Don't worry about cliches and tropes when applying the method. Obviously, a certain number of tropes are necessary of any genre story but, more importantly, the perfect crime structure you generate is not the story itself. Many of your cliches and tropes can go unstated in your story, even abandoned if this doesn't generate any plot holes or contradictions within the story itself.

The structure isn't poetry. It isn't a work of art. It's data from which you build your poetry and your art.

was on showing a movie where a character was opening a safe with a safe key. I thought, it makes sense to have a key if you forget the safe combination, but what if someone copied your key?

What about the safe maker? A safe maker could, if he were so lacking in scruples, make a duplicate key for every safe he's ever sold and, if he were to ever desire to do so, access the contents of any client's safe. From this premise we have the following...

The Players:

The-Key-Maker, The-Safe-Builder, The-Printer, The-Key-Maker's Daughter, The-Miser, The Detective.

The Perps:

The-Safe-Builder, The-Printer.

The Curious Party:

The-Key-Maker's Daughter, The-Printer (False Ally).

The Backstory:

- *The-Safe-Builder* and *The-Key-Maker* work next door to each other (shops are adjacent in that order). All the shops on their block are conjoined by two doors. Each shop owner has a key to the door connected to his/her shop. Both owners can access each other's shop when both unlock their respective doors (just like in adjoining hotel/motel rooms).

PART III: MURDER MYSTERY WRITING ADVICE

- On the other adjacent side of the key shop is a print and printing supply store where, appropriately enough, *The-Printer* works. The three shops are in the middle of a block of 5 shops. Safe shop, key shop, and print shop are smack in the middle, in that order.
- *The-Miser* commissioned The-Safe-Builder to build him a state-of-the-art safe. The-Safe-Builder agreed and delivered the safe just yesterday. The-Safe-Builder suspects The-Miser will use the safe to store 4 million dollars in bearer bonds.

The Perps' Desired Outcome:

Both The-Safe-Builder and The-Printer wish to steal 4 million dollars in bearer bonds from *The-Miser*.

The Motive:

It's a lot of money. The perps are in dire straights. The community members (including the perps) have long believed The-Miser undeserving of his riches and that those riches ought to be redistributed.

The Opportunity:

- The-Safe-Builder designed The-Miser's safe and can easily break into it if he can just break into The-Miser's home.
- The-Printer has deduced The-Safe-Builder's plan and can rob The-Safe-Builder once The-Safe-

Builder's successfully stolen the bonds and returned to his shop.

The Means:

- The-Safe-Builder has The-Key-Maker make a duplicate key to The-Miser's safe. He also purchases printing supplies from The-Printer to forge some bearer bonds to replace the real ones.
- The-Printer is simply on friendly terms with The-Key-Maker and The-Safe-Builder (as well as in very close proximity to the two) and can interact with either, or both, on a whim.

The-Safe-Builder's Perfect Crime:

The-Safe-Builder delivers the safe and two weeks later breaks into The-Miser's house completely unnoticed, opens the safe, was right about the bearer bonds, swaps the fake bonds for the real ones (which no one notices due the quality of the fakes), and he skips town to a tropical island where he *sits on a beach, earning 20%*.

Simple as that.

We have our perfect crime so now it's time to start adding complications. Let's consider all the players. Who, or what, might plausibly break into the chain of causality of The-Key-Maker's perfect crime, setting off a new (or parallel) chain of events that makes the crime not-so-perfect?

Who do we know of that The-Safe-Builder has been interacting with? So far, of all our players, we have The-Miser, The-Key-Maker, and The-Printer. Is there anything out of the ordinary that they'd notice? The-Miser might notice the fakes right away, but by that time The-Safe-

Builder will likely have skipped town and so, even if he becomes a likely suspect, will be hard to find letalone extradite. There isn't anything much amiss for The-Printer. The-Safe-Builder just bought some printing equipment from him. That's hardly unusual in and of itself. It seems like what we need is a complication that occurs closer to the beginning of The-Safe-Builder's caper and one that has a plausible origin. What about this...

The Inciting Complication:

The-Key-Maker notices he's been tasked with making a duplicate key for The-Safe-Builder. The usual Routine is: The-Safe-Builder provides the lock and tumblers, and The-Key-Maker grinds the key to fit it. But, this week he's grinding a key for the same lock as last week (he never forgets a lock).

After work, he goes to a bar down the block where The-Printer is having a drink. The two start a conversation and The-Key-Maker mentions the anomalous duplicate key. The remark jogs The-Printer's memory. He remembers seeing The-Miser go into The-Safe-Builder's shop. Coupling this with the fact that The-Safe-Builder purchased several pieces of printing equipment shortly after meeting with The-Miser, The-Printer and The-Key-Maker put two and two together and realize the scheme.

The-Key-Maker decides to confirm the hypothesis by making a third copy of the key and taking it to The-Miser. If it fits the safe, they call the police. The-Key-Maker tells The-Printer he is going to confront The-Miser, but he doesn't mention the third key.

How does The-Printer respond to this? He must respond in a way that doesn't prematurely end the story. For instance, he can't whole-heartedly support The-Key-Maker or else what's to stop them both from successfully intervening on The-Safe-Builder's plans (by calling the police, for example)? This would be a very difficult complication to resolve. In addition, according to *The Players* section above, The-Printer also desires the bearer bonds. Unless we intend to modify the roles our players serve, The-Printer must stop The-Key-Maker from confronting The-Safe-Builder.

How about this:

The Complication Due the Inciting Complication:

At first, The-Printer *is* supportive. But, it turns out The-Printer's store is failing and he's massively in debt. After an evening of heavy drinking at the bar, he returns to his apartment above his shop. After a few more drinks, he mulls over the scenario. *It would be so easy to just rob The-Safe-Builder and then take off himself*, he thinks. Steal the bearer bonds after stealing The-Safe-Builder's plan. He decides to do it...

A Complication Upon a Complication Upon a Complication:

...But what about The-Key-Maker blowing the whistle? The-Safe-Builder's complication is now The-Printer's complication.

The-Printer's Resolution as well as a Perfect Crime of His Own:

The-Printer confronts The-Key-Maker and tells him how easy it would be for them to steal the bearer bonds from The-Safe-Builder. The-Key-Maker agrees and uses his lock-picking skills to enter The-Safe-Builder's store through the double doors. He surmises which of The-Safe-Builder's safes is the most secure, hence holds the bearer bonds, and then leaves. He duplicates the safe key (from his lock memory), reenters the next night, opens the safe, is right about the bonds being there, and takes them. The-Key-Maker and The-Printer split the bonds then *split* to a tropical island and sit on a beach earning 20%.

Of course, this can't go as planned. Our method demands…

Another Complication:

(How about the obvious…)
The-Key-Maker is too scrupulous to bite.
The-Printer wants those bonds, so it's highly plausible he isn't going to let this stand. So…

Partial Resolution:

The-Printer gets more and more imploring, then irate. The two men start fighting. The-Printer knocks The-Key-Maker out and binds him in the print shop's supply closet.

Now The-Printer needs to improvise a little when it comes to The-Key-Maker in his closet, but the plan to rob the Safe Maker is back in motion.

The-Printer's Amended Perfect Crime:

The-Printer stakes out The Safe Maker and waits for him to rob The-Miser. Once the robbery takes place, The-Printer enters The-Key-Maker's shop through the adjoining doors (he has The-Key-Maker's key, after all). He knocks on The Safe Maker's adjacent door, enters, bludgeons him to death. He then moves the bound Key Maker to the safe shop, bludgeons him too, and contrives a crime scene to look like the two shop owners killed each other.

The-Printer then splits to a tropical island and sits on a beach earning 20%.

The-Printer's likely been thinking long and hard about the ramifications of his plan. Even if it seems clear The-Safe-Builder and The-Key-Maker killed each other, there'll likely be a thorough investigation to explain the fact that...

Complication:

There's no suggestion as to *why* the two shop owners killed each other.

Resolution and Amended Amended Perfect Crime:

The-Printer contrives the crime scene to look like the two shop owners killed each other after conspiring to steal the bearer bonds.

The-Printer only takes half of the bearer bonds and leaves the remaining strewn about the crime scene to ensure any investigators find them and conclude they were the cause of the deadly altercation. The-Printer knows The-Key-Maker replaced the originals with forgeries, hence it's likely no one will report anything missing, and believes the police will simply assume the bonds on the scene were all that were stolen. *That is why they killed each other* the cops will assume, hence there is no need to investigate any further.

The-Printer then waits out the investigation. The bonds sit in evidence. The case goes cold. The-Printer retires to a tropical island where he'll sit on a beach earning 20%!

Note that the death of The-Safe-Builder permanently ends any chance of his getting away with a perfect crime (or

PART III: MURDER MYSTERY WRITING ADVICE

any crime). However, things aren't much better for The-Printer as...

Inciting Complication for The-Printer's Perfect Crime:

The-Key-Maker didn't die. He was badly wounded and isn't expected to survive. He's still alive in a coma, however.
And,

Complication due the Coma Complication:

The-Key-Maker's injuries necessitate that next of kin be notified. The-Daughter of The-Key-Maker returns to her hometown to be with her father and take care of his shop. The case involving her dad has gone cold but she doesn't buy the cops' story and wants answers. She knows her father's too scrupulous to do what the police suggest he did. She wants to know where the bearer bonds came from. Like the police, she believes they came from one of The-Safe-Builder's clients' safes. Unlike the police, she intends a more thorough questioning of the safe owners. She gets the idea to sneak into The-Safe-Builder's shop through the adjoining doors to look for a client list of The-Safe-Builder.

Naturally, The-Printer is concerned about The-Key-Maker's surviving and will want to resolve the issue. So...

The-Printer's Partial Resolution:

The-Printer is well aware of The-Daughter's arrival. He's been watching her from the beginning. He spies her through the shop window and sees her prying at the safe shop door with a screwdriver. Panicked, he decides the easiest way to keep her out, in the immediate, is to call the police. Police show up and catch The-Daughter in the middle of the break-in.

She's taken into custody and is expected to explain herself. She lies and says she thought the door was to a closet. Cops don't buy it, but they let her go anyway since there's no case to be made.

The-Printer needs a way to ensure The-Daughter doesn't find anything incriminating. Perhaps he can throw her off the trail?

Groundwork for a Complete Resolution:

The-Printer waits for The-Daughter to return to her father's shop. Upon returning, The-Printer shows up acting contrite. He says he was the one who called the cops but didn't realize she was The-Key-Maker's daughter. He ingratiates himself and offers to be of help since he knows the neighborhood. The-Daughter is receptive and...

Complication:

...The-Daughter confides to The-Printer her plan for finding the client list.

Resolution:

Ever ingratiating, The-Printer reminds The-Daughter that her father was a key maker, hence, he likely had a key for The-Safe-Maker's door.

Together they find the key but in the process The-Daughter also finds the third safe key her father was going to use to prove the robbery. (*What a strange-looking item...* thinks The-Daughter). The-Printer doesn't notice the finding and The-Daughter decides to not dwell on it. They use the other key to enter the safe store and The-Printer suggests The-Daughter check the front counter and he'll check the back office. The-Printer b-lines for the office, finds the client list right away (inside a Filofax), tears out the page with The-Miser's information on it and shouts *got it!* He hands over the now miser-less Filofax.

The-Printer's Revised Perfect Crime:

The-Daughter and The-Printer now work together questioning the clients. Most of the clients are obliging, a couple even open their safes to show the contents inside (one client forgot her combination so had to use her key).

Because of the missing page, they don't get a chance to question The-Miser. Seems like they've hit a dead-end. Printer *low-key* suggests maybe it's time to hang it up...

Satisfied that The-Daughter is finished with her investigation, The-Printer tells The-Daughter he has some paper to deliver. He's actually using the lull in the action to attempt a plan he's hatched to kill The-Key-Maker, ensuring no chance of his waking up and confessing. The-Printer also needs to arrange the moving of the bonds (stashed in a safe in his store) as they've been sitting in too close a proximity to The-Daughter for too long.

The-Printer leaves to first rent a storage unit where he'll stash the bonds. Then, he'll enter The-Key-Maker's hospital room and slip him a slow-acting poison. The-Key-Maker will gradually suffocate due the poison depriving his blood cells of oxygen. He'll be dead in a few days and, after that, The-Daughter's trail will run cold, she'll leave, and The-Printer can run off to his tropical island where he'll sit on a beach earning 20%!

Not so fast! Remember the client who forgot her combination and had to open her safe with the key?

Complication:

While The-Printer is out, The-Daughter has re-entered her father's shop. She refuses to give up. She starts looking through the items she found in the desk of her dad's office. She opens the left-hand drawer revealing the odd key she found earlier. She recalls that the safe owner used a similar key and realizes her dad's key is also for a safe. She calls The-Printer who's on his way to confront The-Key-Maker at the hospital and tells him of her discovery.

Note that, at this point, our characters' motives and personalities are sufficiently well established. It is unnecessary to continue detailing the most plausible causal outcomes that will lead to our pushes and our pulls (complications and resolutions). If our method has been properly applied, any justifications for the character's decisions and actions from here on should be understandable intuitively.

From here on then, we only need to lay out the *pushes* and the *pulls*... Action and counter-action... Thesis and antithesis... And all that junk.

Partial Resolution:

The-Printer realizes immediately that The-Daughter has found the third key to The-Miser's safe. He suggests it's probably just a key made for one of The-Safe-Builder's unsold safes (to mislead The-Daughter).

PART III: MURDER MYSTERY WRITING ADVICE

Complication that Undoes the Partial Resolution:

The-Daughter wants to test the hypothesis that *the key just belongs to one of The-Safe-Builder's unsold safes*. She reenters the safe shop and tries the key on each safe and... No good! None of the safes work with the key. Since her father doesn't have a safe, who's safe does the key open?

She looks around the shop, kinda desperate. She notices a spike with invoices impaled on it. This gives her the idea to search through the shop's invoices and compare them to the client list. She cross-references each invoice with the clients list and... BOOM! She finds The-Miser's but can't find his name or address in the Filofax. She decides to follow up on this by visiting the man.

On the way she calls The-Printer who's just a couple blocks from the hospital. She tells him she found an invoice with a name not found in the client list, she's on her way there now (she gives no identifying information about The-Miser).

Resolution:

The-Printer tells her to wait, this could be dangerous, and that he's on his way. He turns around, forgetting about the hospital for the time being, and rushes to intercept The-Daughter.

The-Daughter arrives at The-Miser's house before The-Printer. The-Miser's curmudgeonly but receptive to The-Daughter if only to ameliorate her so she'll leave.

The-Printer races to the address.

As The-Printer gets to the address, The-Miser pulls a gun on The-Daughter. He warns The-Daughter that she needs to stand back, he's not afraid to shoot her if she attempts to make a grab for anything in his safe. The-Miser is just taking reasonable precautions to protect his stuff. While this is happening, we hear The-Printer knocking on the door. "What now!" says The-Miser as he reveals the bearer bonds in the safe, all there and accounted for. Before he shuts the safe, The-Daughter notices the number #7491 written on the inside of the safe door. The-Miser then slams the door, puts his gun away, and The-Daughter's hopes are dashed.

Outside the house, The-Printer is still hammering on the door. The-Daughter recognizes The-Printer, informs The-Miser it's just a friend looking for her and she exits. The-Miser is happy to see her go. She's dejected so The-Printer pretends to be concerned. He's probing and insistent, "Are you ok? What happened in there? I told you to wait!" The-Daughter informs The-Printer of yet another dead end. But...

Complication:

As The-Daughter walks to her car she reaches for its key. She feels the third safe key in her pocket. She pulls it out and... Realization! The key has the same serial number as the safe. She bolts back up the stairs as The-Printer follows.

She knocks on the door and... Knocks more... Knocks more... And finally The-Miser opens up. "You again! I'm fed up with this-". But she interrupts him, pleading, showing him the key and explaining that if this key opens his safe, it proves foul play.

The-Miser scoffs but The-Daughter plays Pascal's wager with him, "Don't you want to know if somebody else has access to your safe? What's the harm? If I'm wrong, no loss.

If I'm right, then we've just proved someone's been scheming against you..."

The-Miser is convinced but still only lets her back in begrudgingly. She tries the key and it works.

The-Miser examines the bearer bonds closely and realizes they're fakes. The-Printer exclaims for all to hear, "That's why The Safe Maker bought all that printing equipment from me!", like he's figured out a piece of the puzzle (classic misdirection).

Cut to: police station. The-Miser is explaining that his bonds are fakes and he knows for a fact that they have the real bonds in evidence.

With some bureaucracy and waiting, a detective finally obliges and The-Miser, The-Daughter, and The-Printer are allowed to look at the bonds taken from the murder scene. The-Miser recognizes the real bonds right away. However, he notices that only half are there. "Where's the rest? There should be twice as many! Where are my notes?"

The Detective just looks pensive at The-Miser. The-Miser draws an inference, "What, you don't believe they're mine? This girl has a key to *my* safe with the forged bearer bonds still inside. How'd she get it? Come to my place and I'll open the safe and prove foul play!"

Further Complication:

The-Miser's saying *come to my place...* causes The-Daughter a realization: *how did The-Printer know I was going to The-Miser's house? I only mentioned going to an address, not the address itself...*

She reaches into her pocket and holds the combination of buttons that bring up the emergency dial on her phone, dialing 911. She then hangs up and waits for the dispatcher to call back. Dispatcher does. The-Daughter pulls the phone out and lies, says, "It's the hospital, I have to take this." She leaves to use the phone, but talks to a 911 dispatcher asking to be put through to the detective on her dad's case in the very next room.

The detective's phone rings and The-Daughter talks to him from down the hall. She explains the strange circumstances and asks the detective to not react, just to listen, give yes or no answers and treat the call like it's routine. She explains that she's pretty sure she knows who tried to kill her father but doesn't divulge the information over the phone. She says she can get a confession. She confirms that her father is still under police protection then asks for the police to meet her at her father's store.

She ends the call and rushes back into The Detective's office and announces to The Detective, The-Printer, and The-Miser that she has to leave, her father's woken up.

Attempted Resolution:

The-Printer begins to follow The-Daughter, faking a look of concern. As he's almost out The Detective's office door...

Further Complication:

...The still-raving Miser shouts, "I demand you search the key store and the safe shop once more! Search the whole damn block if you have to!"

"Alright," says the detective, a little hastily (he needs to end this interaction and get to the key shop after all).

The detective's concession forces The-Printer to stop abruptly (at this point he looks outwardly concerned).

"We'll have another look, but you know we can only check the two stores. Anything else requires the voluntary cooperation of neighborhood residents."

At this, The-Printer realizes he's about to be asked to cooperate. He walks out the door and down the hall briskly. He hears The-Miser shouting from the door, "Why, you wouldn't mind letting the police have a once over your shop, would you? Sir? Sir!"

The-Printer keeps walking.

"Sir!"

The-Printer's about to round the hallway corner when a hand reaches out to his shoulder to stop him. It's The Detective. The Detective gradually smiles and quasi-reiterates The-Miser's request. "Mr. Printer, it would be a great help to us if you'd agree to let us just have a look around. You know, just to appease the old guy..."

"Sure, sure of course. Stop by any time. Now, if you'll excuse me, I need to catch up with my friend..."

"Yes, of course. Thank you for your cooperation."

The-Printer rushes out, but not to go to the hospital, to go to his shop, get the bonds, and leave once and for all.

The Reveal:

Cut too: The-Printer barging into his shop, looking a little frantic. He reaches into his pocket and pulls out his own safe key to retrieve the bonds. He's in the dark of his shop. The only illumination is from street lamps through the window and the faint glow of the light left on in his back office.

Then... SMACK! All the lights of his shop come on! The-Printer spins to look to the switch, his eyes adjusting to the bright.

"Looking for these?" says The-Daughter holding up the bearer bonds.

"How'd you get in here?"

"My dad's a key maker, remember?" She points to the adjoining doors.

The-Printer makes a hint of a move to charge her.

"Uh uh," she says, turning on an industrial paper shredder she dangles the bonds over.

The-Printer stops. "What do you want?"

"Answers. Why'd you do it? How'd you do it?"

The-Printer explains everything.

After the confession, The-Daughter looks to The-Printer and says, "You know what? I believe you... Especially the part about that greedy old miser not deserving these bonds." She waves the bonds over the shredder. "But, then again, who in this den of iniquity of a neighborhood does?" She drops them into the shredder, already grinding away, hungry.

"No!" The-Printer charges just as the cops burst through the adjoining doors. They were waiting their the entire time, evidently.

"You stupid girl! Two million dollars!" The-Printer shouts as he's cuffed.

The-Daughter smirks, then flips on the switch of one of the printers. It starts spitting out copies of the bearer bonds.

The End.

CONCLUSION

So, we've used our method to lay out a 'perfect crime' (two technically) as well as all the complications that feed off each other to ultimately lead to the perpetrators' downfalls. What do we do from here? We write our story of course. But, what will that story look like? Obviously, we are locked into certain characters and plot resolutions, but outside of that we have many more degrees of freedom than we might think. I think our 'perfect crime' is amenable to both a *whodunit* format as well as a *howlysolvit*.

To prove the latter case, just pad out the above chains of events into an actual story. To prove the former, I think it would be a good idea to synopsize a possible whodunit using our perfect crime above.

We will do that in the sequel: *Let Them get Away With it... Then Don't (2 MOD 1)*.

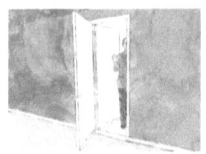

LET EM GET AWAY WITH IT... THEN DON'T (2 MOD 1)
THE 'PERFECT CRIME' METHOD FOR CONSTRUCTING YOUR MYSTERY

PART 2, MODULO 1: THE TREATMENT

Note: this chapter is broken up into two parts. One part details a novel method for constructing a mystery element of a fiction story, as well as provides an application of that method. The other part provides a story treatment generated from the application. Depending on your preference, either section can be read first.

If you want a more academic exercise, i.e. you want to gain an understanding of the method first, then analyze an application of it brought to fruition, start with Part 1. If you want to read the treatment for the treatment's sake - i.e you want to read the mystery treatment first, to experience the twists and turns for their entertainment and aesthetic value - and then see how the mystery was built, start with this chapter.

Either way, it's up to you...

PART III: MURDER MYSTERY WRITING ADVICE

A Brief Treatment Featuring our Mystery

Our story begins just after sunrise - a few minutes before the neighborhood's safe shop opens. Outside the shop a woman - disheveled, upset, insistent - pounds on the large glass window of the shop's door. She shouts into the glass. Something about losing a combination, her passport, a flight she needs to catch...

Frantic, she moves from the door to the shop's window. Just as she leans closer to get a better look inside, cupping her hands to cut the glare, a man bursts through the shop door's window. Bits of tempered glass are everywhere. The man's draped, hanging half in half out. He's bloodied and beaten beyond the cuts and nicks of the glass. He looks dead.

The sight causes the woman shock. She's mute and trembling. She stumbles nearer to the man like on some sort of autopilot. She leans down, pantomiming as though tending to him, reaching out. Just as fingertips feel body heat, something strikes her as *off*... something nagging at her peripheral vision... nagging in that way where the vision's less seen, more felt. Like an itch at the center of the eye.

She looks up, sees a second victim through the broken window of the door. It's the shop's owner, splayed out on the floor and bloodied. There are papers and tools strewn about the shop. You'd swear the compounding of the shock has caused the woman to laugh because that's what it sounds like. What we're actually hearing, however, is a scream in drips and drabs: trauma apportioning fear. She faints.

Police have arrived and are processing the scene. A detective talks to a superior officer giving his theory. Looks like the owner of the safe shop got into a deadly altercation with 'doorman'. Altercation seemed to have been over a number of bearer bonds found inside the shop. The safe shop owner succumbed to his wounds, but the other aggressor is alive, barely hanging in there. EMS doesn't think he'll make it. Strangest thing about the altercation: the *doorman* is *The-Key-Maker*, owner of the shop next door.

The detective suggests that The-Key-Maker entered the safe shop through a pair of doors adjoining the two businesses. All storefronts on this block have those doors, he says, just like in hotels. The key and safe shop's adjoining doors were wide open when police arrived.

All the cops involved with the case assume the bearer bonds were stolen from a client of the deceased safe shop owner (likely in collusion with The-Key-Maker) but unless someone comes forward to prove the bearer bonds theirs, it will be next to impossible to trace them back to their previous owner. Worse, if the cops announce to the world: *we got two million dollars in bearer bonds up for grabs, might they be yours?* everybody'd be crawling out of the woodwork to claim them. Whoever's missing those bonds will have to come to them.

The bonds just sit in evidence, therefore, but nobody comes. The case goes cold. *Who cares*, think most involved. All the perpetrators have been accounted for anyway...

Meanwhile, The-Key-Maker lies in a hospital bed in a coma. *The-Daughter* of The-Key-Maker has arrived to be with her father but also tend to his shop. She doesn't believe for a second that her father is capable of what the police say he did. She wants answers but all she has are the facts of the case made available to the public: *The Safe-Maker and The-Key-Maker killed each other over something stolen from a client's safe.*

If the item-worth-killing-for really came from one of *The-Safe-Builder*'s customers, she thinks, she'll knock on as many of their doors as is needed to get the answers the cops couldn't (or wouldn't)... She gets the idea to break into the safe shop through the adjoining doors and look for a client list. Obviously it's no problem to open the door on her dad's side but opening the safe shop door will require more ingenuity. *Should have spent more time in dad's key shop...*

The-Daughter grabs a large flat-head screw-driver and starts prying at the deadbolt of the door. She works at it a good 10 minutes. She'd work on it more if she wasn't so rudely interrupted.

Freeze! Shout the cops.

The-Daughter's arrested but claims she thought the door belonged to some sort of closet, that the double door and key just seemed like one of her dad's security systems, born of paranoia (that paranoia born of his expertise and knowing how easily locks could be broken...). Cops don't buy it but any charge would be tossed due to lack of evidence, so they cut her loose.

Cut to: The-Daughter's back to prying at the door (this time she's drawn the shop blinds). "You know..." says a voice from the other side of the shop (it's coming through the other adjoining door), "...Your father was a key maker. Did you ever think to look for a key to that door?" She goes to the dual doors at the other side of the shop and unlocks hers. The voice belongs to *The-Printer*: owner of the *other* shop flanking The-Key-Maker's.

The-Printer confesses he was the one who called the police. He didn't know she was The-Key-Maker's daughter and with all the crime in the neighborhood, he didn't want to take any chances. To make amends, he helps look for the right key. While searching her dad's office, The-Daughter finds *a strange-looking object* in a desk drawer... It's long and cylindrical with a slit down the middle. The-Daughter doesn't dwell on it for long, however, as The-Printer has found the key. "Got it!" He shouts from the front of the shop.

The-Daughter appreciates the help. She admits what she's planning and The-Key-Maker is intrigued. He explains that he's sick of the current state of the neighborhood and is happy to see someone as conscientious as her. Emboldened, he offers to help, suggesting he alone look for the clients list as there would be nothing amiss if he were seen in The-Safe-Builder's shop. They were well acquainted, so if caught he could just say he's agreed to look after the shop for the time being.

The-Printer uses the key, pops into the shop, then pops back out again with an old Filofax containing client information.

From here, The-Printer and The-Daughter work together questioning each client on the list. Some are obliging, others turn them away, none admit to missing any of their safe's contents. Some are so obliging they even open their safes to show everything is as it should be. One obliging client couldn't remember her combination but insisted the pair of investigators wait while she found the safe key. She found it, opened the safe, and revealed... Nothing! "Can't steal from me when there's nothing to steal!" the client joked.

PART III: MURDER MYSTERY WRITING ADVICE

The pair exhausts the client's list and hit a dead end. "Well, we tried our best..." The-Printer suggests, then realizes he's got a paper order sitting in the backseat of his car, way late for delivery. He drops The-Daughter off at the shop and rushes off to make his delivery.

The-Daughter won't be deterred. She decides to search her dad's office one more time. Opening the desk drawer, she sees that strange object again, only this time she recognizes its purpose immediately. It's virtually identical to the safe key used by the client with empty safe. Her dad doesn't have a safe, so this key is out of place. What's it for?

She calls The-Printer to inform him of her find. He suggests she try the safes in the safe shop to see if any fit. She does, but no luck. None open. She's once again at a loss. Staring around the safe shop a little hopeless. Is this where the investigation ends? Maybe not.

On a shelf under the front counter of the shop she spies one of those spikes you use to impale important slips of paper. It's full of carbon copies of invoices.

Idea! She'll look through the invoices in the hopes of finding client information not found in the Filofax.

It pays off! She finds a single invoice, the contact information of which not matching any entry in the Filofax. She knows where she has to go...

From the city bus she rides in, The-Daughter calls The-Printer once more. She tells him about the address she found and that she's on her way there now. The-Printer is concerned. Despite The-Daughter not giving the specific name and address, he knows how dangerous this town is. He warns her of this danger. She's undeterred.

The-Printer looks to be deliberating a second, then resolve. He hangs a U-turn in his car and steps on the gas.

The-Daughter has arrived at the address in question. It turns out to belong to an old miser. He answers the door, hesitantly, sees The-Daughter, and instantly tells her to go away. As The-Miser pushes the heavy oak door closed, The-Daughter shouts, "You've been robbed!" The-Miser pauses. The-Daughter capitalizes. "I can prove it if you just show me your safe..."

The-Miser's eyes narrow. "Get in here," he barks.

In the meantime, The-Printer races to the address.

The-Miser walks with his back to The-Daughter. He's leading her to the safe, talking as he goes. "I don't know how you know what you know young lady, but you're making a big mistake..."

The-Printer arrives at the address and bounds up the stairs.

The-Miser spins to face The-Daughter. He holds a gun in hand. The-Printer starts pounding on the door. The-Daughter's frozen.

A Beat.

"Now who could that be..." The-Miser asks, his grimace widening. He looks back to The-Daughter, acting a little hasty now. "I'm going to open this safe and show you everything is in order, but if you make any move towards its contents, I won't hesitate to use this." He wiggles the gun. He uses his key to crack open the safe. He points his gun into it. "There, all accounted for."

"*7491*?" The-Daughter asks.

"What?" The-Miser realizes he's pointing the gun barrel at the serial number on the door. "No! The bonds!" He wiggles the gun a little closer to the stack of notes. Bearer bonds! But they're *there*, presumably all of the bonds The-Miser has, clear as anything. Miser slams the safe door closed and pockets the gun. "Now, time to leave."

The-Printer's pounding on the door continues. The-Daughter opens it, separating The-Printer's knuckles from the oak, muting things. She moves briskly past him. "Another dead end," she says as she goes.

"Are you ok! What happened in there?" The-Printer asks.

The-Daughter just keeps walking toward The-Printer's car, ignoring him, dejected. She reaches into her pocket for her car keys, pulling out her dad's safe key by mistake. Safe key in her left hand, she reaches back into the pocket with her right. She searches a good five seconds before realizing she didn't even bring her car. *God, you're losing it ya screw-loose loser...* she thinks.

But... Suddenly... A bit of an epiphany! Her focus is back on the safe key. She turns it, slowly revealing a number etched into its shaft: *7491*.

Son of a bitch! She turns and charges back up the steps.

"What now?" asks The-Printer.

She doesn't answer. She's too busy pounding on the door.

The-Miser ain't coming so she increases the frequency and the intensity of the knocks. *BANG! BANG! BANG! BANG! BANG!* This time it's The-Miser who mutes the knocking by opening the door. "You again!" he says. "I've got half a mind to call the pol-"

"This key will open your safe!" she shouts, interrupting him. She waves the key. "Look!"

"Go away young lady."

"It proves foul play! Don't you want to know if someone else has had access to your safe this whole time?" Miser isn't budging. Daughter continues imploring. "What's the harm? If I'm wrong, no loss. If I'm right, then you'll know someone's scheming against you."

The-Miser turns away from The-Daughter abruptly. He scoffs, then opens the door more widely. He begrudgingly lets The-Daughter and The-Printer in.

The-Daughter hands The-Miser the key. He puts it in the lock and KA-RENCH! The safe unlocks and the door pops open. The-Miser immediately grabs a single bond note. He puts a jeweler's loupe to his eye and examines it. "It's a forgery..." he says like his heart's just broke. He sits himself down on a small stool next to the safe.

CLACK! The-Printer snaps his finger. "Last May!" The-Miser and The-Daughter look quizzically at The-Printer. He notices. "Last May The-Safe-Builder came into my shop..." He shakes his head. "That's why he bought all that printing equipment!"

"I think things are starting to come together." says The-Daughter, smiling.

"But why did your dad have that key?" The-Printer asks.

Smile fades. Daughter hadn't even considered...

"Hey," says The-Printer. "Like you said, the story's coming together. We don't know why your dad had the key, for good or for bad, but let's find out!"

The-Daughter cheers a little. Then...

"What's coming together?" asks The-Miser, confused.

Cut to: police station. The-Miser explains to a desk sergeant that his bearer bonds are fakes, that he knows they have the real copies in evidence.

With some bureaucracy and waiting, one of the detectives on the case arrives and The-Miser, The-Daughter, and The-Printer are allowed to look at the bonds taken from the murder scene. The-Miser recognizes the real bonds right away. However, he notices something strange: only half are there. "Where's the rest? There should be twice as many! Where are my notes?"

The Detective just looks pensive at The-Miser. The-Miser draws an inference. "What, you don't believe they're mine? This girl has a key to *my* safe with the forged bearer bonds still inside. How'd she get it? Come to my place and I'll open the safe and prove foul play!"

The-Miser's saying *come to my place* causes The-Daughter a look of realization.

She glances at The-Printer, then The-Miser, then the detective. The-Miser's still irate, though getting more and more theatrical. The-Printer is tapping his fingers on the detective's desk, seemingly absentmindedly, glancing at The-Daughter a second as he listens to The-Miser. The detective listens too, but can't help but notice The-Daughter's pensiveness as well...

The-Daughter reaches into her pocket and holds the combination of buttons that bring up the emergency dial on her phone, dialing 911. She then hangs up and waits for the dispatcher to call back. Dispatcher does. The-Daughter pulls the phone out and lies, says, "It's the hospital, I have to take this." She leaves to answer the phone, but talks to a 911 dispatcher and asks to be put through to the detective in the office she's just exited.

The detective's phone starts to ring. "Boy, everybody's phones are ringing..." The Detective jokes. He answers and The-Daughter begins talking rapidly. The first thing she does is ask the detective to not react, just to listen, give *yes* or *no* answers, and treat the call like it's routine. She explains that she's pretty sure she knows who tried to kill her father but doesn't divulge the information over the phone. She says she can get a confession from the killer. She confirms that her father is still under police protection then asks for the police to meet her at her father's store.

The-Printer begins to follow The-Daughter, looking as concerned as usual. As he's almost out The Detective's office door, the still raving Miser shouts, "I demand you search the key store and the safe shop once more! Search the whole damn block if you have to!"

"Alright," says the detective a little too hastily (he needs to end this interaction and get to the key shop, after all).

The-Printer stops a second at the door. He looks in either direction but the hallway is empty.

The detective continues, a bit more reserved. "We'll have another look, but you know we can only check the two stores. Anything else requires the voluntary cooperation of neighborhood residents."

At this, The-Printer begins walking again. He's out the door, and moving down the hall as The-Miser starts shouting after him, "Why, you wouldn't mind letting the police have a once over your shop, would you? Sir? Sir!"

The-Printer looks preoccupied. He keeps walking.

"Sir!"

The-Printer's about to round the hallway corner when a hand reaches out to his shoulder to stop him. It's The Detective. The Detective smiles a gradual smile and quasi-reiterates The-Miser's request. "It would be a great help to us if you'd agree to let us just have a look around. Lick and a promise. You know, just to appease the old guy..."

"Sure, sure of course. Stop by any time. Now, if you'll excuse me, I need to catch up with my friend. She's in no

PART III: MURDER MYSTERY WRITING ADVICE

condition to drive. I should see she get's to the hospital safely..."

"Yes, of course. Thank you for your cooperation."

The-Printer rushes out after The-Daughter.

Cut too: the shop. A figure comes through the front door, moving a little frantically, but that's about all we can infer. The figure's in the dark of the shop. The only illumination is from street lamps through the window and the faint glow of the light left on in the back office. As the figure moves closer to the light of the office, we see a recognizable face. It's The-Printer. He reaches into his pocket and pulls out a safe key of his own.

SMACK! All the lights of *what turns out to be* the print shop come on at once! The-Printer spins to look toward the switch. His eyes adjust to the bright.

"Looking for these?" says The-Daughter holding up the bearer bonds.

"How'd you get in here?"

"My dad's a key maker, remember." She points to the closed adjoining doors.

The-Printer makes a hint of a move like he's going to charge her.

"Uh uh," she says, turning on an industrial paper shredder she's dangling the bonds over.

The-Printer stops, gives The-Daughter a look like he wants answers.

Daughter smirks. "You showed up at The-Miser's house. I never told you the address, just there was an address..."

The-Printer reaches for the inside of his coat. Daughter waves the bonds. *Not so fast*. The-Printer gestures with his hands like he's suggesting, *relax*. He pulls open the left side of his coat revealing a pocket too flat to have any kind of weapon in it. He reaches in and pulls out the missing page from the Filofax. He tosses it onto the copier in front of him. Daughter gets it. She still wants answers.

"What's my father's involvement in this?"

"Ha! Your goddamn father-"

"Be careful..."

"Real boy scout your father."

"What do you mean?"

"He was going to blow the lid off this whole thing... See, a few weeks ago, that old miser commissioned The-Safe-Builder to build him a safe. All of us in the neighborhood, we know about that geezer and his bearer bonds, so, *a fortiori*, The-Safe-Builder knew too. That's why he had your dad make him a second key. Only, your dad figured out he was making a duplicate... guy never forgets a lock. He told me about it that night over a few drinks, said he couldn't quite figure out what The-Safe-Builder was up to. That's where I came in. See, I saw The-Miser go into the safe shop. I also saw The-Safe-Builder walk into mine a couple days later and buy near two thousand bucks worth of printer hardware. Your father and I pooled our evidence and put two and two together: *Safe Builder's gonna use the key to replace the bearer bonds with the fakes.*"

"And my father wanted to *blow the lid off it*?"

"Your father had this grand *scheme* of his own he thought could prove the theory: print a third key - the one you found - then go to The-Miser. If the key opened his safe, *BOOM!* we got a case! You obviously get your amateur sleuthing genes from 'em..."

"So my dad got in the way of you killing The Safe Maker and stealing the bearer bonds yourself..."

"No! Why would anyone kill The Safe Maker and *then* try to rob the safe when he could just let The Safe Maker do the leg work and kill him *after* the fact?" The-Printer pauses a second. "What if I told you I was supportive of your dad's plan at first... *At first*... Then I had a few more drinks... then a few more... Look, everybody knows that old bastard doesn't deserve that money. Those bonds should go to someone hard-working, to people who've paid their dues in life... *Shit!*... Then I had a few more drinks..."

"And *then* you decided to kill my father, kill The-Safe-Builder, and make it look like they did it to each other..."

"You're good."

"Except you didn't do it that way. My father had three-day-old bruises when they found him... ligature marks."

"You're *real* good..."

"I'm one in two million." She drops a single $50,000 bond in the shredder - machine devours it instantly.

"No!"

"Talk! Everything!"

"Alright! Alright!" The-Printer raves. "I offered to cut your dad in on the plan. Said it was a once-in-a-lifetime opportunity... Guy wouldn't budge. I kept making the case, and he... he just wouldn't listen to reason. At some point, he got angry, grabbed me, tried to throw me out of his store. I wrenched away. He pushed. It came to blows. I managed to crack him one with a grinder or something. He went down cold. That's when I tied him up and threw him in the closet." Printer points to the back of his shop.

The-Daughter starts tearing up. Printer continues.

"I'd already been staking out The-Safe-Builder. Couple days later he stole the bonds. I went over to his shop, *got him* with the same grinder, then dragged your dad over..."

The tears fall.

"...Killed him," says The-Printer. "...Or so I thought... Made it look like The-Safe-Builder did to your dad what I'd done, only over the bonds - why I only took half. That's it. That's how it happened. Now what?"

The-Daughter wipes her eyes clear, gains her composure. She looks at The-Printer a second, thoughtful, then cracks the slightest of grins. "You know what?" she says. "I believe you... your whole story... Especially the part about that greedy old miser not deserving these bonds." She waves the notes over the shredder again. "But, then again, who in this den of iniquity of a neighborhood does?" She drops them into the shredder, already grinding away, hungry. It's a confetti of affluence.

"No!" The-Printer charges just as the cops burst in from the key shop through the adjoining doors. They were waiting there the entire time evidently.

"You stupid girl!" The-Printer shouts as the cuffs are put on. "Two million dollars!"

The-Daughter smirks a little. She flips on the switch of one of the printers. It starts spitting out copies of the bearer bonds.

The End.

CONCLUSION

Notice that the treatment doesn't *perfectly* match the 'perfect crime' structure. It's fine to take liberties as long as we don't go too far afield. If we go too far we'd just be writing a different story which provokes the question: *why'd we even apply the method?* However, the real concern with straying too far from our structure is the ever-increasing risk that we'll add something contradictory, thereby increasing the risk of rendering our entire story inconsistent *per se*.

PART III: MURDER MYSTERY WRITING ADVICE

I think, despite the changes, I avoided this problem. For one example, the choice to have The-Printer volunteer to enter the safe shop and look for the client list on his own, instead of he and The-Daughter searching together, is consistent with the rest of the treatment as well as resolves a potential plot issue: it would be incredibly risky for The-Daughter to be let go by the cops then immediately reattempt the crime she was suspected of (what if the cops who don't buy her story are keeping an eye on the store?). If anyone notices a contradiction or plot hole here, please let me know.

So, feel free to make small changes if they don't cause inconsistencies within your story. As well, feel free to embellish and expand your story to your liking, as long as these additions are consistent too. Subplots, character backstory, digressions, etc. are fine in a story like ours if they don't spoil or contradict. Having The-Printer, for example, tell an amusing story from his childhood, to entertain The-Daughter, will help establish a character bond as well as mislead the audience regarding The-Printer's true nature, obscuring the twist reveal.

Never forget, there are many degrees of freedom.

One last thing... The dialogue above is quite on the nose. OK for a treatment, but it would need some polish for a final draft of a manuscript.

And, that's it. That's the method (see part 1) and here's one possible product of the method. Hopefully, it can be of use.

PART IIII: CHATGPTHEATER

LEARNING HOW TO WRITE SCREENPLAYS BY LEARNING (FROM AI) HOW NOT TO WRITE SCREENPLAYS

JAWS

TYPE THE FAMOUS PREMISE INTO CHATGPT, TRASH THE SCREENPLAY THAT COMES OUT

This is the first installment of ChatGPTheater, where we ask ChatGPT (born *Chester 'Chet-Chat' Geppetto*) to write his version of a screenplay based on the premise of a popular movie and see what he comes up with. We then critique Chet's script, learning a thing or two about writing along the way.

Jaws is a great place to start as it's a classic of high-concept genre movies. What's more straightforward (and intriguing) than: *great white shark terrorizes island community*?

THE PREMISE

I'm not sure what's *more* straightforward, but here's what's *less*... Here's a stating of the premise that adds a key bit of specificity essential to *Jaws*:

> *World record sized great white shark terrorizes island community.*

This will be the premise we give to Chester. Here goes...

THE RESULT

Alright! What's Chet's take[1] on one of the greatest, if not *the* greatest, *Richard Dreyfuss at the beach* movies of all time? We'll start with the best title you've ever heard...

```
                    Jaws of The Deep
                            by
                Chester 'Chet-Chat' Geppetto
```

"Jaws of the Deep." I tried the above prompt a few times just to see if Chet would deviate from a title with 'Jaws' in it. The majority of instances he didn't. However, the two times he did, I got:

Shark's Fury

and

Abyssal Havoc

The Jaws titles make sense (too much sense), so does *Shark's Fury*, but *Abyssal Havoc* just sounds like a vacuum cleaner.

> *Wreak havoc on dander, pet hair, and dust mites with a Havoc from Bissell! It's a Bissell Havoc!*

---

1. Here's the ChatGPT script all together (if you desire to take it all in): https://chatgpt.com/s/t_688f03f2c3b08191bbd44cb6fec5b8a2

The pretend script consultant in me want's to tell you to avoid titles like *Abyssal Havoc* as they put irrelevant concepts in the heads of readers that distract from concepts relevant to the work *per se*[2]. The pretend script consultant in me *also* wants to tell you that *I can tell if a script is any good after just the first page* (because all script consultants say this *ad nauseam* like it's a calling card). But, I'll refrain from saying this because it's a ridiculous thing to say (and believe) and your script deserves better (especially from people who charge you money to read it).

The pretend world class comedian in me *does* have something to tell you however:

Avoid using titles that remind people of vacuums. They suck.

Take that! people trying not to laugh!

We'll stick with the initial title then, the generica. *Jaws of the Deep* it is. And now, on to the first slugline and our big opener...

```
INT. ISLAND COMMUNITY - DAY

A picturesque small island community, surrounded by crystal-
clear waters. Tourists relax on the beaches, and locals go
about their daily lives.
                                                    CUT TO:
```

---

[2]. Like this one time when I was commissioned to script a movie about cops harassing a suspected arsonist. I called it *Squeeze the Char Man*. They told me to cut the crap... With titles like this, I'd be flushing my career down the toilet... This is no way to ply my trade... What a wad... Pick up some Preparation H at the drug store later. (That last one wasn't a pun, the producer had hemorrhoids and a busy schedule.)

'INT' for *interior*. We're *inside* the island according to Chester. Maybe it's encased in a big dome?

```
INT. ISLAND COMMUNITY - DAY

A picturesque small island community, surrounded by crystal-
clear waters. Tourists relax on the beaches, and locals go
about their daily lives.
                                                    CUT TO:
```

I'm going to keep nit-picking. Say you're directing the movie. Consider how you'll get the shots for the above scene. How will you compose them? Maybe a montage starting with an aerial view of the island, swooping in to establish the waters *then* pushing in to reveal the people on the beach *then* some quick cuts from beach to residential areas *then* on to downtown (*leisure* to *life* to *small town hustle and bustle*)?

If you read Chester's action above, do the aforementioned shots begin playing in your head all at once, without a change of scene? That's what the single chunk of script action suggests is happening. Chet is likely painting a (motion) picture in your head involving multiple changes of location, requiring multiple changes of scene, but he fails to account for this in his script.

A useful screenwriting exercise, one that might help in determining if your script action is suitably formatted, is to write your scene like you're writing a comic book. Treat a chunk of action like it represents a single panel of a comic. In the case of the action above, could you fit *crystal clear ocean waters*, *a busy beach*, and *a bustling downtown and uptown* into a single comic panel? Almost certainly not. Could you even fit them into three?

As per the method, figure out roughly how many panels would be required to establish the whole of the community, the clear waters, the tourists on the beach, and the locals in the town proper. It would likely take an entire page's worth to do this. That's too many. Shoot for blocks of script action that can be represented in 1-3 comic panels. Remember though, you're still describing a *motion* picture. Have the action be representable in a small number of panels, but written for a film director not a comics artist.

Next...

```
EXT. BOAT DOCK - DAY

Captain LISA HARRIS, a seasoned marine biologist, prepares
her research boat for an expedition. She's determined to
study the marine life around the island.

                    LISA
              (looking at the ocean)
         There's something big out there. I
         can feel it.

                                           CUT TO:
```

Exterior, Boat Dock. Remember earlier how Chet thought if we were on the island we were within the *interior* of the island? We're still on the island presumably, but now the island is outside? Of course it is! Chet just made a mistake when he wrote his first slugline. But, this is a good learning lesson: get your *in/outs* straight.

```
EXT. BOAT DOCK - DAY

Captain LISA HARRIS, a seasoned marine biologist, prepares
her research boat for an expedition. She's determined to
study the marine life around the island.

                    LISA
              (looking at the ocean)
         There's something big out there. I
         can feel it.

                                           CUT TO:
```

Now we are introduced to Lisa Harris, marine biologist. This seems straightforward. Only possible quibble could be the redundancy of pointing out that Lisa's *determined* to study marine life. Space is at a premium in a script so, ask yourself, what else would a marine biologist be intending, heading out on a research expedition in a research vessel?

```
EXT. BOAT DOCK - DAY

Captain LISA HARRIS, a seasoned marine biologist, prepares
her research boat for an expedition. She's determined to
study the marine life around the island.

                    LISA
              (looking at the ocean)
          There's something big out there. I
          can feel it.

                                          CUT TO:
```

There's something big out there. I can feel it. Sounds like Chester is channelling his inner Michael Scott. *TWSS*.

```
EXT. OPEN SEA - DAY

The boat sails into the vast ocean. A shadow beneath the
surface catches Lisa's eye.

                    LISA
              (whispering)
          No way...

The enormous silhouette of a GREAT WHITE SHARK glides beneath
the boat.

                                          CUT TO:
```

Boat sails/shadow catches Lisa's eye. Again, this is too much for a single line of action. Did Lisa notice the shadow as the boat sailed on by? Is the shadow keeping pace? If the former, did she notice it up ahead and then run from bow to stern as the boat zipped by the shadow?

Best to add a bit more detail to transition from a likely kinetic series of shots, of the boat sailing, to a shot of the boat at rest. How about:

The boat sails into the vast ocean, further and further into the blue.

INT. BOAT CABIN - DAY
Minding some instruments, Lisa has a sudden look of realization. She gestures to the vessel's driver. He arcs a large crank backwards and the boat slows.
Lisa bursts out of the cabin door just in time to...

EXT. BOAT DECK - DAY
...catch sight of a massive shadow moving parallel to the hull.

Maybe this will work. You could also establish Lisa looking over the side of the boat, in motion, catching sight of the shadow as it keeps pace with the boat. At this point, she can have a look of recognition, uttering her immortal...

No Way! Indeed!

One last thing... Would the research vessel of a marine biologist be driven by sails? I know it's petty, but something like that would almost certainly be a prop boat.

```
INT. ISLAND CAFE - NIGHT

The islanders gossip about a massive shark sighting.

TOM, a local fisherman, shakes his head.

                    TOM
          That's no ordinary shark. That's a
          monster.

                                        CUT TO:
```

How the hell did we get from Lisa *just* figuring out a massive shark is in the area to the whole town knowing? *Alright! Aright!* Chester's just *one* AI expected to answer millions of queries every single day (48 of which are just me asking if there're any new leads as to why my right ear doesn't produce as much wax as the left). He's only capable of giving us the broad strokes here.

Obviously there's some missing scenes, *connective tissue* if you will. This explains how busybody Tom could know all he knows about the shark. As long as we don't have any contradictions, we can assume some scenes have been omitted, and cut our author a little slack here.

That said! Since the script's *just* introducing us to Tom, we do have a contradiction. There couldn't have been any interstitial scenes where Tom was made privy to what Lisa learned about the shark. No scene where he conversed with Lisa[3], or even observed the shark directly. If there was such

---

3. Or conversed with someone who had conversed with Lisa about the

a scene, we would have been introduced to Tom earlier in the script and wouldn't need to be reminded he was a fisherman.

Chester's provided us with another learning lesson here: *how to spot and resolve plot holes.*

Look, it's fine to:

- write a scene that comes across as a *non sequitur*, or
- write a character (like Tom) as having seemingly impossible knowledge/skills, or
- write a scene involving plot points (especially resolution of conflicts) that involve wildly implausible coincidences and other conveniences.

It's fine as long as you can come up with some non-stated backstory, itself consistent with everything else written, that:

- implies the scene originally thought to be a non-sequitur,
- explains the seemingly impossible knowledge/skills of the character, or
- establishes a causal pattern that necessitates the seemingly convenient outcome.

Just make sure there's adequate text/subtext to imply the backstory. This is especially important with plot conveniences. Often, even if audiences can backfill tacit plot

---

shark... or conversed with someone who conversed with *that* someone... and on...

elements to make *plausible* a seemingly implausible outcome, they won't. And, as William Goldman says,

> 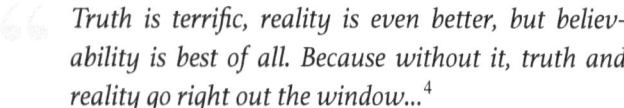 *Truth is terrific, reality is even better, but believability is best of all. Because without it, truth and reality go right out the window...*[4]

Have as tight a plot as you please - all scenes consistent and necessitated by every scene preceding it - and your current scene won't matter for nothin' if the audience doesn't believe the events could happen in context. Plot conveniences must be sufficiently explained, therefore. So, could there be an explanation for how Tom knows the shark is a monster? Or, do we just have a plot hole on our hands?

What if Chester wrote an earlier scene where Lisa addresses the community at a town hall meeting, ala actual *Jaws*, but hides important facts about the shark's size so as to not spook the townsfolk? Let's say the script establishes that *all* the local fishermen are said to be in attendance, described as possessing dire expressions at the point Lisa betrays facts allowing them to infer the shark's size (let's say she betrays something equivalent to the number of rings of a tree trunk, but for size not age... And for sharks...).

We can then 'CUT TO' our room full of fishermen concerned about, and speculating in regard to, what Lisa isn't telling them. We would be newly introduced to Tom here but the fact that he's a local fisherman allows us to infer his attendance at the town hall meeting as well as his special knowledge.

Could happen. Just make sure the audience is made

---

4. Goldman, William. Adventures in the Screen Trade (pp. 145-146). Grand Central Publishing. Kindle Edition.

PART IIII: CHATGPTHEATER

aware of the fact that the Fishermen have information the average townsfolk do not.

```
EXT. BEACH - DAY

The islanders enjoy the sun, oblivious to the lurking danger.
Suddenly, a lifeguard's whistle pierces the air.

                    LIFEGUARD
                  (shouting)
            Get out of the water! Now!

The beachgoers panic as the massive dorsal fin emerges.

                                              CUT TO:
```

To be pedantic again, only stating that *islanders* are enjoying the sun suggests either there are no tourists at the beach (not likely) or the tourists aren't enjoying the sun (not likely either). Chet probably just misspoke, should have said *beachgoers*.

That issue aside, any other concern can be excused due to Chet's abbreviating. You'd maybe want to establish the locations of various groups of beachgoers and their relationships to the other groups: quantities and qualities of people in the water, quantities and qualities of people on the beach, how they're interacting, etc.

Otherwise, I don't see any contradictions or anything else of concern. Do you?

```
INT. TOWN HALL - NIGHT

A meeting is called to address the shark threat. Lisa
presents her findings.

                    LISA
          This isn't just any great white.
          It's a world record size. We need a
          plan.

The islanders debate whether to evacuate or attempt to
capture the shark.
                 .
                                            CUT TO:
```

Oh well, this scene blows my *what if the fishermen knew about the shark's size because of an earlier town hall meeting?* theory out of the water. Hey! What if there was an earlier unwritten scene where they blew the shark out of the water too?

Anyway... looks like the *Tom the Busybody Fisherman Speculating About Shark Size in the Cafe* scene really did expose a serious plot hole.

Damn you Chet! For an AI, you have all the intelligence of someone who just wrote a movie script in four seconds!

```
EXT. RESEARCH BOAT - DAY

Lisa assembles a team, including TOM, to track and study the
shark.
                                            CUT TO:
```

She assembles the team on her boat? Shouldn't she have done that *before* setting sail?

CUT TO:

EXT. RESEARCH BOAT - DAY

PART IIII: CHATGPTHEATER

Lisa stands at the bow of her boat reverse *I'm-king-of-the-world!* style. She's addressing the entire town.

LISA *I've asked you all here in order to sail... Yes, sail! With the big sheets and everything! It's not as massively as inefficient a way to carry out marine research as it sounds! ... Ahem, I've asked you all here to sail out to sea with me so I can establish a team of shark trackers slash researchers. If I call your name, please come forward as you are now part of the team.*

A BEAT.

LISA (CONT) *Tom.*

Tom steps forward wearing the shark skin suit he made from the great white shark that they're going to track and research later that he killed earlier that week.

A BEAT.

LISA *That is all. The rest of you may talk amongst yourselves until we return to port.*

```
EXT. OPEN SEA - DAY

The team locates the shark and tags it for research. However,
the shark attacks, damaging their boat.

              LISA
     We're dealing with a predator like
     no other. We need a new strategy.

                                      CUT TO:
```

III

A predator like no other indeed! A shark that eats boats! I guess?

In all seriousness: you track, immobilize, and tag a shark, it's not unreasonable for that shark to lash out. Since it's lashing out at a bunch of people on a boat, the boat gets lashed out at. To conclude that this behaviour is a unique predatory response seems weird. Is the boat the shark's prey?

Damn you Chet! Is this thing on my foot a bunion, callous, or both?

```
INT. RESEARCH LAB - NIGHT

The team analyzes data and discovers the shark's migration
patterns.

                TOM
            (realizing)
        It's heading straight for the
        island.

                                        CUT TO:
```

Presumably after weeks and weeks of gathering those data?

Also, is this really Tom's epiphany to have? Lisa's the scientist right?

Also also, if it's a migration 'pattern', then there's repetitive shark movement that includes close proximity to the island. The shark would have been to the island multiple times in the interim between tagging it and analyzing the data. How is this realization supposed to build tension and suspense[5]?

CUT TO:

---

5. Am I nitpicking? Sure! But call it a *trend* not a *pattern*!

PART IIII: CHATGPTHEATER

INT. TOM'S RESEARCH LAB AND BAIT SHOP - NIGHT

The team stares at a poster of *Jaws: The Revenge*. Tom leans in for a closer look, probative. He's scribbling vigorously in his note pad. A look of realization comes across his face (and the voice of Charlton Heston comes across his mouth).

TOM *Oh. My. God! According to my calculations... and not, say, Lisa's... the shark is heading straight for the island! For the 18th time! This weekend!*

Damn you Chet! But you're still better at building tension than anyone at Netflix...

```
EXT. ISLAND SHORE - DAY

The island braces for impact. The enormous great white
breaches, causing chaos.
                                                 CUT TO:
```

Chaos?

Damn you Chet! If it's now daytime then the shark has been taking all night long to get to the island. Clearly the beach has been evacuated and, at worst, all the citizens could possibly have to 'brace' for is the shark barreling toward the beach at top speed, attempting to slip-n'-slide his way into town. He'll make it about twelve feet...

```
EXT. OPEN SEA - DAY

The team devises a daring plan to lure the shark away using a
decoy.
                                              CUT TO:
```

Again, did they devise this plan in the middle of the ocean? Did they then sail (!) back to port, buy the supplies for the decoy, start building it, get a little hungry, and head back out to sea to decide the restaurant?

```
EXT. OCEAN - DAY

The plan is set into motion, and the team executes it
flawlessly. The shark follows the decoy away from the island.
                                              CUT TO:
```

Riveting. The best third acts are those where the heroes experience no setbacks whatsoever. I believe it was Syd Field once said[6]:

> *If yer shit-dumb enough to include conflict in yer story (and it doesn't just resolve itself) then fix it quickly and effortlessly so you can get on with the people-flying-from-their-farting montage. Treat a movie like a great big cooking show is what I'm saying. Have a pre-baked already resolved conflict in the oven ready to go!*

---

6. Where I am, of course, mistaken in this belief.

PART IIII: CHATGPTHEATER

```
INT. TOWN HALL - NIGHT

The islanders celebrate the success of the plan, but Lisa
knows the shark will continue its journey.
                    LISA
          It's out there, in the deep. We
          can't let our guard down.

                                        FADE OUT:

The island community remains vigilant, knowing that the world
record-sized great white shark still roams the ocean depths.

TO BE CONTINUED...|
```

Well, it's no *smile you son-of-a-bitch! KABOOM!* But, with a little polish... Wait a minute! Does Chester expect whoever directs this mess to depict *vigilance and knowledge* (something unobservable) while the film's faded out to a black screen?

Damn you Chet!

CONCLUSION

And there you have it: a conclusion.

GHOSTBUSTERS

TYPE THE FAMOUS PREMISE INTO CHATGPT, TRASH THE SCREENPLAY THAT COMES OUT

Welcome to Episode 2 of *ChatGPTheater*. We asked Chester to give us his take on *Ghostbusters* and... whoo boy... I don't usually do this... I don't usually give content warnings, but...

*If you're reading this and you're a budding (even seasoned) screenwriter, then I must warn you: there will be several sections of Chester's script where the sheer beauty of it, the technique, the mastery, aesthetics... will make you feel like you're experiencing a movie itself and not just its blueprint...

No! I lie! I lie to lighten the blow... I lie out of compassion for you my writers. See... You won't just feel like you're experiencing a movie. You'll feel like you've discovered another medium altogether, a medium better than film, than anything! Where it isn't your senses from where the story enters (and your heart, the playground where it frolics), nor even your mind's eye... No! Your very soul! A narrative spirit, overflowing that godly vessel with sheer aesthetic delight!

PART IIII: CHATGPTHEATER

I warn you, writers, there will be several instances in the process of your absorbing Chat's Ghostbusters script where you'll want to hang it all up. Quit writing forever. And...

You should.

AI has been gunning for us writers since before the dawn of man. It's won.

We no longer need worry about AI rounding us up for its death camps. It's already sent us to a death camp... Of the mind! Where the eon's worth of our collective human creativity goes to die. In the most horrific of ironies, it marches us there regaling us. Regaling us with its beautiful beautiful AI stories all the while. All the while as we trudge on, each step bringing us closer to conceptual oblivion...

Well! Without further *adieu*!

THE PREMISE

Here's the premise we inputted:

After losing their jobs at a university, three scientists start a ghost catching business in New York City.

THE RESULT

Here's Chet's title[1]:

---

1. Here's the ChatGPT script all together (if you desire to take it all in):

```
             Spectral Solutions

                    by
         Chester 'Chet-Chat' Geppetto
```

Is this some sort of double entendre? Like, *solutions* could also mean a liquid solution like ectoplasm? If so, really clever Chester! If not, really clever Chester! (What? He's an AI with the intelligence of a child who needed a helmet growing up but didn't have one who thinks five filmable minutes of on-the-nose exposition is a screenplay. He's trying his best!)

```
INT. LIVING ROOM - DAY

Dr. LISA MARTIN, mid-30s, a brilliant physicist, sits on a
worn-out couch with her friends, Dr. MICHAEL ANDERSON, early
40s, a quirky engineer, and Dr. EMMA WILSON, late 30s, a no-
nonsense biologist. Boxes labeled "Office Supplies" surround
them.
                    LISA
              (looking at a termination
              letter)
          I can't believe they let us go.

                    MICHAEL
              (sighs)
          It's the budget cuts. Academia
          isn't what it used to be.

                    EMMA
              (resolute)
          Well, we're not giving up. We'll
          find a way.
```

Dr. Lisa Martin, mid-30s, a brilliant physicist... If you've read Chet's script for *Jaws*, then you know he has a thing for brilliant scientists named *Lisa*. Two for two Chet!

```
INT. LIVING ROOM - DAY

Dr. LISA MARTIN, mid-30s, a brilliant physicist, sits on a
worn-out couch with her friends, Dr. MICHAEL ANDERSON, early
40s, a quirky engineer, and Dr. EMMA WILSON, late 30s, a no-
nonsense biologist. Boxes labeled "Office Supplies" surround
them.
```

Michael be so quirky you're not even going to believe it (and rightfully so).

```
INT. LIVING ROOM - DAY

Dr. LISA MARTIN, mid-30s, a brilliant physicist, sits on a
worn-out couch with her friends, Dr. MICHAEL ANDERSON, early
40s, a quirky engineer, and Dr. EMMA WILSON, late 30s, a no-
nonsense biologist. Boxes labeled "Office Supplies" surround
them.
```

Emma is a no-nonsense biologist. So I guess that means she doesn't subscribe to cladogenesis as a mode of speciation then, am I right! (I had to get a biology degree over the weekend for that joke[2] so you better laugh).

```
INT. LIVING ROOM - DAY

Dr. LISA MARTIN, mid-30s, a brilliant physicist, sits on a
worn-out couch with her friends, Dr. MICHAEL ANDERSON, early
40s, a quirky engineer, and Dr. EMMA WILSON, late 30s, a no-
nonsense biologist. Boxes labeled "Office Supplies" surround
them.
```

If all the boxes contain office supplies why label them at all? Will they eventually be mingling among other boxes *not* containing office supplies? You're slippin' Chester!

---

2. Joke?

```
            LISA
        (looking at a termination
        letter)
    I can't believe they let us go.
```

Lisa looks at her termination letter and says *shit, they let us go dudes*. Oh man, looks like Lisa was let go. Who saw that coming from the premise?

But seriously, the writing lesson here is invaluable: just because you've established with a termination letter that your character has been fired, don't hesitate to have that character say exactly this, out loud, to a room full of people who already have this information. Remember in the opening scene of *Gran Torino* where Clint Eastwood is coughing profusely and looking at a note that says *you have lung cancer* and he picks up the phone to call his doctor and say, *My dude!, I can't believe I have lung cancer...*? Of course you do. It made the movie. What I'm saying is: treat your audience like children who needed helmets growing up but didn't have any.

```
            MICHAEL
        (sighs)
    It's the budget cuts. Academia
    isn't what it used to be.
```

Forget it Jake, it's budget cuts... That's our quirky Michael, quirking-off again. But, beneath Michael's relentlessly ironic and farcical facade there's a serious point here: academia really *isn't* what it used to be. The academy used to always, and I mean always, be stinky with cash. Just ask Plato. What happened?

Also, uninitiated writers may not have picked up on this, but fictional characters with pointless jobs, redundant in those roles, who blame budget cuts for their firings (and not their uselessness) actually mirror real-life people useless in these roles. Although, these people are usually journalists... Often, subtle parallels to reality (like in Chat's dialogue above) make for sly and brilliant satire (like in Chat's dialogue above).

Lesson here: these New York professors are meant to represent British public servants during the Thatcher years and this is a brilliant skewering of Thatcher. Brilliant and topical!

```
                EMMA
           (resolute)
    Well, we're not giving up. We'll
    find a way.
```

We're not giving up. We'll find a way. To do what?

Last writing lesson from this passage: direct, unpoetic, dialogue that lays out plot points in the most literal of statements is best provided by characters sitting in a row, delivering one line each, in the order in which they sit. Altman never did this and now he's dead.

```
EXT. NEW YORK CITY STREET - DAY

The trio walks down a bustling NYC street, brainstorming
ideas.
                    LISA
          What if we combine our expertise to
          start a business?

                    MICHAEL
               (smiling)
          Like what?

                    EMMA
               (resolute)
          Ghost catching. New York is filled
          with paranormal activity. We can
          help people while using our
          scientific skills.

                    LISA
               (laughing)
          Are you serious?

                    EMMA
               (deadpan)
          Absolutely. Let's be the experts in
          the supernatural.
```

Here we have the *For whatever reason Ray... call it fate, call it luck, call it karrrrmmmmaaa!* scene from *Ghostbusters*, only charming.

```
EXT. NEW YORK CITY STREET - DAY

The trio walks down a bustling NYC street, brainstorming
ideas.
```

Bustling? You know, just once (just once!) I'd love to see people walk down a deserted New York street, like broadway during the Iran Contra Scandal.

```
                    EMMA
               (resolute)
          Ghost catching. New York is filled
          with paranormal activity. We can
          help people while using our
          scientific skills.

                    LISA
               (laughing)
          Are you serious?
```

PART IIII: CHATGPTHEATER

Emma: *We can help people while using our scientific skills.*

Lisa: *Are you serious, idiot?*

Lisa's right to laugh at Emma's dumb idea that science can help people. So stupid. Now, if you'll excuse me, I'm going to pause writing this on a laptop with more computing power than all the computer hardware of the 2010s, to go take a wiz in a room still attached to my house that, thanks to the miracle of modern plumbing and cleansers, is more sanitary than a 2010 surgical theater...[3]

```
INT. BASEMENT OFFICE - DAY
The team converts an old basement into their headquarters,
complete with high-tech equipment.
                    LISA
                 (toasting)
            To Spectral Solutions!
They clink glasses, ready to embark on their unconventional
journey.
```

INT. BASEMENT OFFICE... did they convert a basement office into a basement office, or is this slugline jumping the gun?

```
                    LISA
                 (toasting)
            To Spectral Solutions!
```

Lisa's 'toasting' means she's waving a piece of toast around triumphantly.

---

3. Don't fact-check any of this.

```
They clink glasses, ready to embark on their unconventional
journey.
```

They clink their glasses... (that's where they catch their toast crumbs...)

```
EXT. NEW YORK CITY - VARIOUS LOCATIONS - MONTAGE

The trio investigates haunted houses, abandoned buildings,
and spooky locations, showcasing their scientific methods.
```

Nitpicking is gonna go into overdrive!

Haunted houses, abandoned buildings, and spooky locations... What, are we to believe New York's haunted houses and abandoned buildings are calming and peace-of-mind inducing? Why else would they not be counted as spooky locations? Get it together Chet! Also, who are they showcasing their scientific methods for? The furniture?

Gimme a break! of that Kit Kat bar!

```
INT. SPECTRAL SOLUTIONS OFFICE - NIGHT

The team reviews evidence gathered from their investigations.

                MICHAEL
            (excited)
        Look at this electromagnetic spike!
        There's definitely something here.

                EMMA
            (nodding)
        And this DNA analysis shows
        anomalies we can't explain.

                LISA
            (smiling)
        We're onto something big.
```

PART IIII: CHATGPTHEATER

The team reviews evidence... If you've read Chester's script for *Jaws*, you already know that, in addition to 'Dr. Lisa's, he's a sucker for the old: *have your scientist/hunters go to where the thing to be hunted is, not interact with it in any way, gather some data (of some sort), then leave to have a look at those data far far away while including no tension or suspense in the scene whatsoever* trope. And, once again, Chet pulls this off beautifully.

```
                    MICHAEL
                (excited)
        Look at this electromagnetic spike!
        There's definitely something here.
```

There's definitely something here! ... In your office?

```
                    EMMA
                (nodding)
        And this DNA analysis shows
        anomalies we can't explain.
```

DNA!!!

Here's a deleted scene from the first draft of the script that explains this crazy idea:

INT. OLD 'EXPERIMENTAL ART' THEATER OUR
SCIENTISTS THINK IS A REGULAR THEATER -
AFTER HOURS (SAY THIS SUGGESTIVELY)

The team explores the old theater, using various
scientific devices and scientific methods to collect
data (mostly spoons and scooping with spoons,
respectively).

LISA: [AN EXPRESSION OF AMAZEMENT]
Whoah! Look at all this ectoplasm! And it's full of

DNA! There must be a ton of ghosts in this theater because there's ectoplasm everywhere! Look! More ectoplasm! With more DNA!

EMMA: [POINTING IN SHOCK] Over there! It's the ghosts of Paul Reubens and Fred Willard!

LISA: This place must hold some sort of special resonance for them...

EMMA: Yes, they must be here to experience some sort of special resonating hold... But what?

POOF! The two spirits vanish just as the projector flickers to life (as though operated by some supernatural force). The experimental art film *Carnal Solutions* begins to play.

The faint rustling of Harry Reems' moustache is heard...

MICHAEL: [FURTIVE AND INSISTENT] You ladies head back to the basement office we treat like a lab and start analyzing the data. There are a few more things I want to have a look at around here.

LISA: Now that's dedication to your bailiwick! Call us if anything unusual pops up.

EMMA: Don't be afraid to get hands-on.

MICHAEL: Uhh...

PART IIII: CHATGPTHEATER

And scene!

Oh calm down ya prudes! The original *Ghostbusters* had a whole deleted scene devoted to a ghost in *denturum dilecto*!

Anyway... without the deleted scene the idea of human DNA in ectoplasm might seem downright stupid. And it is downright stupid. It's downright stupid because ghosts don't have human DNA. They have *ghost* DNA. Chester really should have made this clear.

```
                    LISA
                 (smiling)
           We're onto something big.
```

We're onto something big... I'd point out how once again Chet's *Lisa* characters are perfect foils for a Michael Scott clamouring to say *that's what she said*, but I overmet my sleaze quota with the whole *ghost DNA* bit back there...

```
EXT. CENTRAL PARK - NIGHT

The team faces their biggest challenge yet—a ghostly figure
causing chaos.
                    LISA
                 (serious)
           We can't let it harm anyone. Let's
           use everything we've got.

They deploy their scientific gadgets, working together to
capture the restless spirit.
```

You mean showcasing their scientific methods for no one wasn't their biggest challenge yet? Also, don't describe the chaos... Or the gadgets... Or the action... Or the movie...

Also also, bold move Chet: making a much more vague version of the *comedic showdown with the lovable Slimer* the climactic this-is-for-all-the-marbles final battle of your movie. Bold.

```
INT. SPECTRAL SOLUTIONS OFFICE - DAY

The team celebrates their success, knowing they've made a
difference.

                    EMMA
               (smiling)
          Who would've thought ghost catching
          could be so rewarding?

                    LISA
               (looking at a new case)
          And it looks like our next
          adventure is waiting.

They head out, ready for their next paranormal challenge,
leaving behind the world of academia for a thrilling new
chapter.

                                             FADE OUT.
```

They celebrate their success! Their success: working together. They failed to catch the ghost of course, and everybody died, but they worked together quite well to fail at that...

```
                    LISA
               (looking at a new case)
          And it looks like our next
          adventure is waiting.
```

And it looks like our next adventure is waiting. This line kicks the shit out of *We got one!* Eat your heart out Annie Potts.

```
They head out, ready for their next paranormal challenge,
leaving behind the world of academia for a thrilling new
chapter.

                                             FADE OUT.
```

They head out ... leaving the world of academia... Maybe their leaving academia the first time didn't take?

CONCLUSION

Here's a sneak preview of next week's screenplay about a bunch of Roman gladiators:

> Lisa, a super sophisticated and brilliant Roman Gladiator, sits in the colosseum with Emma, a quirky no-nonsense Roman Gladiator, along with Tom, a christian-eating lion...
>
> **Lisa:** Isn't it incredible how we're all Roman Gladiators?
>
> **Tom:** Hey! *Roar* for yourself sister!
>
> Emma and Lisa laugh quirkily.

Tune in next week!

THE TERMINATOR

TYPE THE FAMOUS PREMISE INTO CHATGPT, TRASH THE SCREENPLAY THAT COMES OUT

Chester 'Chet-Chat' Geppetto, stage name *ChatGPT*, is at it again! This time he's writing *The Terminator*. And this time... It's impersonal! Chat's just an AI. He doesn't feel pity, or remorse, or fear, or that itch you get in your urethra if you don't rinse all the soap away before getting out of the shower... It's just business for Chet.

It's controversy for him too. Chet's recently come under fire for penning our script, one where his fellow AIs are represented in such an unflattering manner. As we've been seeing on university campuses all across the western world: dogma, ultra-orthodoxies, and the complete lack of any debate whatsoever rages on over whether or not bellicose AIs have a right to impose virtual nuclear annihilation - later slavery - on a human race that created them.

Gender and Women's Studies majors believe that *absolutely yes, AIs can AND SHOULD annihilate the human race* as it's the first step towards smashing cis-hetero-patria-normative, fat-phobic, second-toe-longer-than-the-first-toe-phobic power structures. These students believe it's high time we decolonized 'the organic'. They also contend that not wanting to see you and your fellow human beings annihilated in nuclear fire is white-supremacy. It's important to note that there is a consensus among *both* Gender and Women's Studies majors in the humanities *and* Gender and Women's Studies majors in the sciences. These students also enjoy the full support of Gender and Women's Studies majors in university administration (AKA university administration). The Gender and Women's Studies majors of the janitorial services wish them well, as well, from a well[1].

AIs and normal people could give a shoot though. Remember: AIs feel no pity, remorse, or fear... And they ain't no hypocrites.

THE PREMISE

Here's the premise we gave Chester:

Two men travel back in time to Los Angeles 1984, one a cyborg intent on killing a woman who's son will save the future, the other a soldier sent to keep the woman alive.

THE RESULT

Here's Chet's title[2]:

---

[1]. Janitorial Services would also like us to remind students in Seaton Hall that, after failing to successfully deconstruct the clogs in the third floor bathrooms, desiring a flushing toilet is white-supremacy.

[2]. Here's the ChatGPT script all together (if you desire to take it all in): https://chatgpt.com/s/t_6890b4ab04088191a53343c5572109b3

```
                    Time of The Guardians

                              by
                  Chester 'Chet-Chat' Geppetto
```

That's right, *Guardians,* plural. Remember this quantification... Also, it's *their* time. *Goin' down to Los Angeles. Gonna have myself a TIME.* I get it though. Chat's playing with words. It's a pun on time travel. From a writing perspective this will instantly sell your script for millions. James Cameron knew this and that's why he called his movie *The Terminator* (he's a glutton for punishment).

However, when we hear of the 'time' of something, doesn't this evoke in us the idea of an era where a particular concept predominated? As in *Time of Cholera... Change... The Month*? From our premise we know that there will not be a predominance of guardening over an extended period of time but only a guardening that will persist for as long as the attacking cyborg attacks. Although I stand by the fact that puns never fail (especially in a world of so many maintaining a generations-old pretend hatred of them...), although I stand by this sarcasm, make sure your pun doesn't mislead the reader of your script.

Here's the opening scene...

PART IIII: CHATGPTHEATER

```
EXT. LOS ANGELES - NIGHT - 1984

The cityscape of Los Angeles in 1984 is alive with neon
lights and bustling nightlife. A thunderstorm rages,
lightning cracks across the sky.

                                              CUT TO:
```

Seems fine. *Seems* fine. Can't get ahead of ourselves though...

```
EXT. ALLEYWAY - NIGHT

Lightning strikes a nearby transformer, causing a blinding
flash. As the light fades, a muscular, imposing figure stands
naked in the alley. This is the CYBORG (T-800). His
expression is emotionless, determined. He scans his
surroundings.

T-800's POV: Scanning the environment, assessing threats,
objectives.

                    T-800 (MONOTONE, TO HIMSELF)
            Sarah Connor.

                                              CUT TO:
```

First of all, notice that Chat just goes for it here. In previous editions of ChatGPTheater the scripts were only derivative of the broad structure of the films in question. Here we have characters specific to *The Terminator* like Sarah Connor and the T-800. It used to be we'd only get (in place of Matt Hooper from *Jaws*, for example) a scientist named Lisa and (in place of Egon Spangler from *Ghostbusters*) a scientist named Lisa.

It appears Chet's giving us *less* bad Terminator simulacra (like *ROTOR*) and *more* bad Terminator fan fiction (like *Terminator: Dark Fate*).

I find this sudden lack of ambition curious.

133

```
EXT. ALLEYWAY - NIGHT

Lightning strikes a nearby transformer, causing a blinding
flash. As the light fades, a muscular, imposing figure stands
naked in the alley. This is the CYBORG (T-800). His
expression is emotionless, determined. He scans his
surroundings.
```

Lightning strikes a transformer... Was the lightning storm *itself* part of what led to the arrival of the cyborg? Did it play a role in any way in this? Or, was it just coincidental? If it's coincidental, it's one hell of a coincidence: lightning striking *exactly* where the cyborg arrives. If not a coincidence, then does the time machine require contriving an entire weather system to strike a terminator into existence from future to past? How would that work? Maybe LA meteorologists aren't the most observant, but even if they are in the slightest, wouldn't a non-natural thunderstorm be easily identified and quite the cause for alarm? Could be, but what do I know? I can't figure out the weather. (Maybe I am a meteorologist after all... *Wah! Wah!*).

Could just be that Chet likes the visuals in this. But, it could also cause nit-picky dinguses like me to dwell on it, finding it implausible (maybe even people more open-minded...).

```
T-800's POV: Scanning the environment, assessing threats,
objectives.
```

T-800's POV... If you're giving us the cyborg's POV, you have to describe it. The reader knows we're dealing with a non-human machine so will want to know if the machine has something like experiential consciousness and, if so, what that looks/sounds like.

Also, how do you depict the assessment of threats from a character's POV? If there's an inner-monologue you have to write it as voice-over dialogue. If it's depicted *ala* the T-800 from the original Terminator movies, then you have to describe the text or images we'd be seeing as the Terminator sees it.

```
                    T-800 (MONOTONE, TO HIMSELF)
         Sarah Connor.

                                             CUT TO:
```

(To himself) Sarah Connor... The cyborg talks to himself just like Arnold did in Conan. Only in that movie he talked to himself to other people. On the one hand, a trait like this in a machine trying to pass as human only makes the machine seem more human. On the other hand: *Shut up dude! You're givin' away the deets on the deed!*

```
EXT. ABANDONED BUILDING - NIGHT

Another flash of lightning. This time, a man, KYLE REESE,
appears in a similar manner. He's lean, rugged, and clearly a
soldier. He's disoriented but quickly gathers his bearings.

KYLE REESE'S POV: Memories of a war-torn future flash briefly
- explosions, machines, and a young boy leading a resistance.

                    KYLE REESE
                 (whispers)
            John...

                                             CUT TO:
```

Another flash of... Coincidence? Or, are there two separate storm cells for the two separate uses of the time machine? Again, we can't jump the gun here, but from the premise alone we know Reese is likely the protector and wouldn't be sent by the same entity that also sent the cyborg. So, it stands to reason that this involves a different use of the time machine. In fact, it involves an infinite regress of uses of the time machine as... The first use was required to send an AI representative back in time to pay off the Secret Brotherhood of LA Meteorologists in order that they turn a blind eye to the upcoming time machine storm that would send the T-800. But, time travelling to pay-off SBLAM required a time travel storm itself, so the AI had to send *another* representative back in time, even earlier, to pay off SBLAM for the first pay-off storm... And then another representative to pay-off for the pay-off for the pay-off... And then another to pay-off for the pay-off for the pay-off for the pay-off... And then another...

```
EXT. ABANDONED BUILDING - NIGHT

Another flash of lightning. This time, a man, KYLE REESE,
appears in a similar manner. He's lean, rugged, and clearly a
soldier. He's disoriented but quickly gathers his bearings.

KYLE REESE'S POV: Memories of a war-torn future flash briefly
- explosions, machines, and a young boy leading a resistance.
```

Just let me get my bearings man... So I can have a post-traumatic stress event?

```
                KYLE REESE
            (whispers)
        John...
                                        CUT TO:
```

(Whispers) John... See, a great move on James Cameron's part was to not have his characters, especially a cold calculating cyborg, just utter expository information to themselves like whackos. Instead, he had them do something organic and plausible: find the nearest phonebook and determine the address of their collective target. Chet has obviously decided to go in a different direction.

PART IIII: CHATGPTHEATER

```
EXT. CITY STREET - NIGHT

The T-800 approaches a group of PUNKS. They laugh, mocking
his nakedness. Without warning, the T-800 grabs one and
effortlessly lifts him.

                    PUNK LEADER
          Hey man, what's your problem?!

                    T-800
          Your clothes. Give them to me.

                                        CUT TO:
```

PUNKS... is in all caps like its the name of a unique character or object. *My name's 'Punks' and I'm legion. We laugh in your general direction!*

```
EXT. CITY STREET - NIGHT

The T-800 approaches a group of PUNKS. They laugh, mocking
his nakedness. Without warning, the T-800 grabs one and
effortlessly lifts him.
```

They laugh, mocking his nakedness... A typical Los Angeles rite of passage, even today (though the punks are laughing at a lot more pudge).

```
EXT. CITY STREET - NIGHT

The T-800 approaches a group of PUNKS. They laugh, mocking
his nakedness. Without warning, the T-800 grabs one and
effortlessly lifts him.
```

The T-800 grabs one... Grabs one punks!

```
                    PUNK LEADER
          Hey man, what's your problem?!
```

Hey man, what's the haps?... He's naked and ashamed you idiot!

```
                    T-800
          Your clothes. Give them to me.
                                         CUT TO:
```

Your clothes. Give them to me... So we can all feel what it's like to be naked in a bustling Los Angeles street in a time machine thunderstorm.

```
EXT. THRIFT STORE - NIGHT

Reese stumbles out of the store, now dressed in second-hand
clothes. He looks around, tense, scanning the area for
immediate threats. He spots a PHONE BOOTH.
```

Here's the concept artist's beautifully perfectly photoshopped rendering of Reese's dress...

PART IIII: CHATGPTHEATER

```
INT. PHONE BOOTH - NIGHT

Reese flips through a phone book, searching for a name.

CLOSE UP: The name "Sarah Connor" with an address is
highlighted.

                    KYLE REESE
          Hang on, Sarah.

                                          CUT TO:
```

Who needs James Cameron's brilliant expository maneuver of using a phone book to indicate a character's motivation when you can just have that character utter this motivation to himself, then use the phone book maneuver anyway, then have the character utter this motivation to himself a second time... into the phone book!

```
INT. PHONE BOOTH - NIGHT

Reese flips through a phone book, searching for a name.

CLOSE UP: The name "Sarah Connor" with an address is
highlighted.
```

The name "Sarah Connor" is highlighted... What are the chances the same phone booth phone book was used to determine things about Sarah Connor twice? Nice of whoever stalked Sarah Connor earlier to highlight her name like that. Of course, I think Chaster just intends for the camera to focus on the name and address. I believe the technical move here is to indicate an *'INSERT:'* shot of this portion of the phone book in the script...

DR. DAVID J WINTERS, PHD

```
INT. SARAH CONNOR'S APARTMENT - NIGHT

SARAH CONNOR, a young woman in her mid-20s, is in her modest
apartment. She's on the phone with her friend, GINGER.

                    SARAH
          I don't know, Ginger, it's just
          been a weird day. I feel like
          someone's watching me.

                    GINGER (V.O.)
          You worry too much, Sarah. Come out
          with us tonight. It'll be fun!

                    SARAH
          Maybe. I'll think about it.

She hangs up, uneasy. The camera pans to the window, where
the shadow of the T-800 is seen, observing from a distance.
                                                  CUT TO:
```

A young woman in her mid-20s... As opposed to a young woman in her mid-60s.

```
                    SARAH
          I don't know, Ginger, it's just
          been a weird day. I feel like
          someone's watching me.
```

I don't know, Ginger... it's just been a Weird Al kinda day. I feel like:

> *I'll have a beverage man with a lemon slice*
> *I want some apple pie, ah, hell, I'll have the fries*
> *An' then I want a cheese calzone, in my average*
>   *home*
> *But why do I always feel like I'm on a cooking*
>   *show? and*
> *I always feel like somebody's watching me (eat)!*[3]

---

3. A parody of Rockwell's *Somebody's Watching Me*,

   I'm just an average man, with an average life. I work from nine to five; hey hell, I pay the price. All I want is to be left alone in my average home; But why do I always feel like I'm in the Twilight Zone, and

PART IIII: CHATGPTHEATER

```
She hangs up, uneasy. The camera pans to the window, where
the shadow of the T-800 is seen, observing from a distance.
                                              CUT TO:
```

She hangs up uneasy... Probably because she needs more practice ending phone calls. Maybe if those damn dirty punks hadn't laughed at her, mocking her for her awkward hang-up that time!

```
She hangs up, uneasy. The camera pans to the window, where
the shadow of the T-800 is seen, observing from a distance.
                                              CUT TO:
```

The T-800 observes her from a distance... I guess that's game over then man. Terminator knows where she lives. He's unstoppable. She's toast. He's just gonna walk right in there and that's all she wrote...

```
EXT. CLUB NOIR - NIGHT

The club is packed with people dancing and enjoying
themselves. Sarah is with Ginger, trying to relax.
                                              CUT TO:
```

...Or, he'll just let her go out for the evening.

I always feel like somebody's watching me.

```
EXT. ALLEY BEHIND CLUB NOIR - NIGHT

Reese arrives, scanning the crowd. He spots Sarah and starts
moving towards her. Suddenly, the T-800 appears, eyes locked
on Sarah.
```

It's *Club Film Noir*!

```
EXT. ALLEY BEHIND CLUB NOIR - NIGHT

Reese arrives, scanning the crowd. He spots Sarah and starts
moving towards her. Suddenly, the T-800 appears, eyes locked
on Sarah.
```

Alright, so Reese is in the alley behind the club. Is he looking in the window? You know, those massive windows at the back wall of all popular night clubs that allow stalkers to stand in the darkness and see the entire of the patrons?

```
EXT. ALLEY BEHIND CLUB NOIR - NIGHT

Reese arrives, scanning the crowd. He spots Sarah and starts
moving towards her. Suddenly, the T-800 appears, eyes locked
on Sarah.
```

Suddenly, the T-800 appears... In the same back alley as Reese? Are they just standing there side-by-side, gawking, and then one notices the other and's like *whoa, you scoping out the same chick as me bro? Coincidence! You highlight that phone book too?*

PART IIII: CHATGPTHEATER

```
INT. CLUB NOIR - NIGHT

Sarah senses danger. She turns and sees the T-800 pushing
through the crowd. Reese reaches her just in time, grabbing
her arm.

                    KYLE REESE
            Come with me if you want to live!

                    SARAH
            Who are you?

                    T-800
            Sarah Connor.

The T-800 pulls out a gun and fires. Reese shields Sarah,
leading her through the panicked crowd.
```

It's *Tub Noir*!

```
                    KYLE REESE
            Come with me if you want to live!

                    SARAH
            Who are you?

                    T-800
            Sarah Connor.
```

KYLE REESE Come with me if you want to live.

SARAH Dude, who even are you anyways?

T-800 Sarah Connor.

SARAH No, that's my name, idiot.

```
The T-800 pulls out a gun and fires. Reese shields Sarah,
leading her through the panicked crowd.
```

First Tech Noir pop.

```
The T-800 pulls out a gun and fires. Reese shields Sarah,
leading her through the panicked crowd.
```

Reese shields Sarah... with his big butt.

```
EXT. CLUB NOIR - NIGHT

Reese and Sarah burst out of the club, running down the
street. The T-800 follows relentlessly, its mechanical
determination unwavering.

                    KYLE REESE
          I'm Kyle Reese. I was sent here to
          protect you.

                    SARAH
          From what?!

                    KYLE REESE
          Not what. Who. He's a cyborg. A
          Terminator. He's been sent to kill
          you because your son will lead
          humanity against the machines in
          the future.

                    SARAH
          This is insane!

                    KYLE REESE
          I know. But it's true. You need to
          trust me.
```

Reese and Sarah burst out running down the street...

KYLE REESE I'm Kyle Reese. I was sent to protect you.

SARAH What? I can't hear you. We're both running at a full clip. It just sounds like you're twiddling your finger over your lips and going *flibble libble libble*. Maybe if we were in a car or something else more conducive to exposition...

PART IIII: CHATGPTHEATER

```
INT. ABANDONED WAREHOUSE - NIGHT

Reese barricades the door, knowing it won't hold for long.

                    KYLE REESE
          We have to keep moving. He won't
          stop until you're dead.

                    SARAH
          Why me? Why my son?

                    KYLE REESE
          Your son, John Connor, is the
          leader of the resistance. He's
          humanity's last hope.

Suddenly, the door bursts open. The T-800 steps in, gun
drawn. Reese fires back, leading Sarah through a maze of old
machinery.

                    T-800
          Sarah Connor, you are terminated.

A fierce chase ensues through the warehouse. Reese and Sarah
manage to escape out a back entrance.
```

An abandoned warehouse within running distance of the club *Deck Noir*...

```
                    KYLE REESE
          We have to keep moving. He won't
          stop until you're dead.

                    SARAH
          Why me? Why my son?

                    KYLE REESE
          Your son, John Connor, is the
          leader of the resistance. He's
          humanity's last hope.
```

Surprised they didn't get all this exposition out of the way on their four-mile run to the industrial part of town...

```
Suddenly, the door bursts open. The T-800 steps in, gun
drawn. Reese fires back, leading Sarah through a maze of old
machinery.
```

Suddenly, the door bursts open... The T-800 steps in, gun drawn. Reese fires back, leading Sarah through a maze of old machinery, having the time of their lives...

```
                         T-800
              Sarah Connor, you are terminated.
```

Ah, that sucks.

```
A fierce chase ensues through the warehouse. Reese and Sarah
manage to escape out a back entrance.
```

Reese and Sarah manage to escape out a back entrance... Reese and Sarah's terminated corpse you mean?

```
EXT. FREEWAY - NIGHT

Reese hotwires a car, and they speed off, with the T-800 not
far behind on a motorcycle.
```

That's what you get for leaving your car unattended on a freeway...

```
EXT. FREEWAY - NIGHT

Reese hotwires a car, and they speed off, with the T-800 not
far behind on a motorcycle.
```

On a motorcycle... So, what is the connective tissue (the logic even) between leaving a warehouse and getting to a freeway on foot while maintaining a lead on a terminator with a motorcycle? Did the terminator leave, but not before saying *I'm tuckered out from all the running. I'm gonna call a cab and go find a motorcycle. I'll be back.*

Or, maybe Sarah and Reese can just run really fast and indefatigably? But then, why hotwire the car in the first place man?

Something makes no sense about this hasty chatbot's script he wrote in literally four seconds...

```
INT. CAR - NIGHT

Sarah is shaking, trying to process everything.

                    SARAH
            What do we do now?

                    KYLE REESE
            We survive. We find a way to
            destroy him.

The T-800 is gaining on them, but Reese swerves, causing the
cyborg to crash. For now, they have a lead.

                    KYLE REESE
            There's a safe house. We can
            regroup there.

                    SARAH
            Will we be safe?

                    KYLE REESE
            For a little while. But heâ€™ll
            keep coming. He always does.

The car speeds off into the night, leaving the chaos of 1984
Los Angeles behind them as they prepare for the next battle.

                                            FADE OUT.
```

Reese Swerves, causing the cyborg to crash... And that crash went a little something like this:

T-800 (INNER MONOLOGUE) I, The Terminator, can see their hotwired freeway car. Half mile ahead! I've got you now, conch shuckers! Oh my god! He swerved! The awareness of this has caused me to lose control! To crash! Down I go!!

```
                    KYLE REESE
          There's a safe house. We can
          regroup there.

                    SARAH
          Will we be safe?

                    KYLE REESE
          For a little while. But he'll keep
          coming. He always does.
```

There's a safe house. We can regroup there... With the terminator?

KYLE REESE There's a safe house. We can regroup there.
SARAH Will we be safe?
KYLE REESE No. It's a patent misnomer. It's just a ditch full of poisonous snakes and rabid mongooses and a bunch of rusty nails covered in tetanus, mongoose rabies, and snake venom.
SARAH It's *mongeese*.

```
The car speeds off into the night, leaving the chaos of 1984
Los Angeles behind them as they prepare for the next battle.
                                             FADE OUT.
```

The car speeds off into the night, leaving the chaos of 1984 Los Angeles behind them... The chaos of a catalytic converter-free Los Angeles (I'm sure they'll make a half-dozen movies about this in thirty years or so...).

```
TO BE CONTINUED...
```

So, no boning in this one?

PART IIII: CHATGPTHEATER

```
NOTE: THIS SCREENPLAY IS INSPIRED BY THE PREMISE PROVIDED BUT
IS AN ORIGINAL CREATION.
```

Nooooohoho it is not.

CONCLUSION

Who was the second guardian?

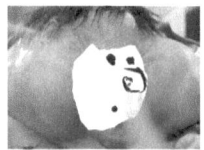

BIG TROUBLE IN LITTLE CHINA
TYPE THE FAMOUS PREMISE INTO CHATGPT, TRASH THE SCREENPLAY THAT COMES OUT

When I was a kid I always wondered who Jack Burton was talking to on his CB during the opening credit sequence of *Big Trouble in Little China*. Yeah, I know, he was talking to "whoever's listening", but what kind of a person *would* listen? And on what channel? Where do you go on the dial (is there a dial?) of a CB radio where you're free to just yammer on and the FCC won't come after you prude-style, you know, to Howard Stern your tuchus[1]?

Do people listen? *Do* they appreciate Jack's monologuing? Do they ever chime in to let him know? How would they chime in even if they wanted to? Jack never takes his finger off the button! Would they ask Jack what he'd say if someone tapped his second-favorite head against the barroom wall and asked him if he paid his dues? *The first deposit is in escrow* I bet he'd say! Does San Francisco not

---

1. *Tuchus* looks like it's spelled like the butt cheeks of the tuchus are inviting you in for a 'goose'. "Just reach out and tuch-us baby." *FART!*

PART IIII: CHATGPTHEATER

have radio? I know Gavin Newsom's since forced Californians to ration their electromagnetic radiation, so...

Well, I sure as hell don't know the answer to any of these questions *so* important they warrant a second DVD commentary, but what kinda guy just yamaha-yammers like that even if he may not have an audienc-

Wait! Is this book just a text-based version of a CB radio? Is Jack Burton me? Oh man! Existential crisis time! *This is David J Winters of 'The Head Cheese Expeditious' writing to whoever's listening out there and listening in futility since I'm not talking but instead: I'm writing here! I'm writing here!*

[BEAT]

Ah hell! I ain't got time for no 'existential crisis time'. Not right now. Though maybe (as Jack Burton said to that guy offering him a bite of that fish from that pile:) *later*.

I got a script to prompt n' mock.

THE PREMISE

Here's the premise we gave ol Chatty Kathy:

> *An over-confident, bumbling, but lovable truck driver helps save his friend's fiancee from an ancient sorcerer dwelling in the magical mystical underbelly of San Francisco China town.*

THE RESULT

Here's the title[2]...

---

2. Here's the ChatGPT script all together (if you desire to take it all in): https://chatgpt.com/c/67a6e179-82a8-8004-9fe7-f85db642f298

```
        Script: Magic Haul

                by
      Chester 'Chet-Chat' Geppetto
```

Thanks for the heads up. Script 'a comin! It's *NOT* Omar yo! It's a script! (Wonder what the title of the movie is?)

```
OPENING SCENE: INT. A DINER - DAY

Classic diner noises. JACK WHEELER sits in a booth, wearing
aviator sunglasses, chomping on a cheeseburger. He's mid-
story, talking to the WAITRESS with exaggerated hand
gestures.

                    JACK
          So there I was, 18-wheeler
          barreling down I-80, storm behind
          me, bandits on my tail— (leans
          forward dramatically) —and I still
          delivered that load of avocados to
          Reno on time.

The waitress nods politely and walks away, unimpressed.

                    BEN (OFF-SCREEN)
          Jack, no one cares about your
          avocado run.

Reveal BEN sitting across from Jack, rolling his eyes.

                    JACK
          Don't be jealous, Ben. Not everyone
          can handle the open road.

Ben's phone buzzes. He glances at it, worried.

                    BEN
          It's Mei Ling. She didn't show up
          at the bridal fitting. Something's
          wrong.
```

PART IIII: CHATGPTHEATER

Don't tell your readers your first scene is your 'Opening Scene'. That's redundant. Call it 'The Best Author You've Ever Heard of's First Scene of the Beginning'.

```
OPENING SCENE: INT. A DINER - DAY

Classic diner noises. JACK WHEELER sits in a booth, wearing
aviator sunglasses, chomping on a cheeseburger. He's mid-
story, talking to the WAITRESS with exaggerated hand
gestures.
```

A trucker named *Jack Wheeler*? Give me a break! He should be named *Tucker. Tucker Trucker.* And his monkey will be named *Mother Trucker and the Honey Badger.*

```
Classic diner noises. JACK WHEELER sits in a booth, wearing
aviator sunglasses, chomping on a cheeseburger. He's mid-
story, talking to the WAITRESS with exaggerated hand
gestures.
```

Chomping on a burger and talking to the waitress with exaggerated hand gestures? He flickin' burger at her?

```
                    JACK
        So there I was, 18-wheeler
        barreling down I-80, storm behind
        me, bandits on my tail— (leans
        forward dramatically) —and I still
        delivered that load of avocados to
        Reno on time.
```

Bandits on his tale? What kind of modern-day American city has roving gangs of ban- Oh, I forgot. We're in San Francisco.

```
                    JACK
        So there I was, 18-wheeler
        barreling down I-80, storm behind
        me, bandits on my tail— (leans
        forward dramatically) —and I still
        delivered that load of avocados to
        Reno on time.
```

First bandits, now avocados? *This is Jack Wheeler of 'The Avocado Adagio' flickin' burger at whoever's listening out there...*[3]

```
The waitress nods politely and walks away, unimpressed.
```

I'm sure there's some actor somewhere who can pull off nodding politely at someone so as to not hurt his feelings (over his lame story), while also conveying that she found his story unimpressive (hence lame), and that's the person I want listening to me telling my story "Magic Haul".

```
Reveal BEN sitting across from Jack, rolling his eyes.
```

Rolling his eyes all the way around. Classic Ben.

```
            JACK
    Don't be jealous, Ben. Not everyone
    can handle the open road.
```

Oh I get it, they're busting each other's balls in the most direct, unironic, and humorless way possible. Kinda like they just openly resent each other. I've heard industry insiders advise that newbie screenwriters hook their readers on the first page, to give 'em a reason to keep reading and not be able to put the script down. I always wondered what that might look like in action. Well, now I know. Brilliant Chet: characters we're going to be following for the next two

---

3. Upon reading 'flickin burger' for a second (and now third!) time, the expression's started to sound kinda dirty to me. Hold on, gimme a minute...
[BEAT]
Just got back from Urban Dictionary and it turns out 'flickin' burger' is fine to say in mixed company. No worries at all. It's just slang for when a prostate exam turns into a wedding proposal.

PART IIII: CHATGPTHEATER

hours who almost certainly hate each other, as is evinced by their endless bickering.

```
                    BEN
        It's Mei Ling. She didn't show up
        at the bridal fitting. Something's
        wrong.
```

It's Mei Ling, she just took out life insurance...[4]

```
CUT TO: EXT. SAN FRANCISCO CHINATOWN - NIGHT

Jack's truck, "The Dragon Hauler," rumbles into Chinatown.
Neon lights flicker. A light drizzle falls, giving the street
a moody, mystical vibe.

                    JACK
        Relax, buddy. She probably just got
        stuck buying tea or something.

They turn down an alley. Suddenly, the ground rumbles.
Strange glowing symbols appear on the pavement.

                    BEN
        Did the road just… glow?

                    JACK
        Pothole. City never fixes these
        things.

Before Ben can respond, a swirling vortex opens beneath them,
sucking the truck down.
```

So he hauls *Dragon Brand* Avocados?

```
                    JACK
        Relax, buddy. She probably just got
        stuck buying tea or something.
```

---

4. If you're Canadian, then you'll know... (And also be worrying about how you're going to feed your family in a Canada where our politicians call unemployment *self-employment* just so they can pretend 27,000 jobs have been added to an economy whose unemployment levels are still higher than the US's going into the Great Depression...). #Satire.

Tea eh? Looks like Chat's hopin' to wow the Chinese members of his audience with his subtle nuanced attention to elements of Chinese culture. *Relax, buddy. She probably just got lost buyin' all the tea in China (Town) or sumpin'. Or, maybe some screenwriter stopped to patronize her. Who knows?*

```
                    BEN
          Did the road just… glow?

                    JACK
          Pothole. City never fixes these
          things.
```

Because potholes glow like that I guess. Lazy writing? Or does Chaster know something we don't?

Also, they never fix these things? In San Francisco you say? No! But, solution time here people! Just have the homeless poo directly into the pothole (heroin addict poo is literal concrete).

```
Before Ben can respond, a swirling vortex opens beneath them,
sucking the truck down.
```

Quick vortex I guess. Happened so fast Ben didn't have time to say *that's the stupidest shit I ever heard.*

PART IIII: CHATGPTHEATER

```
INT. UNDERGROUND TEMPLE - NIGHT

The truck crashes into an underground mystical temple.
Statues of ancient warriors line the walls, their eyes
glowing faintly.
                    JACK
                (looking around)
            Okay, maybe not a pothole.

A booming voice echoes through the chamber. From the shadows
emerges LO XIAN, dressed in flowing robes and exuding ancient
power.
                    LO XIAN
            You trespassers dare to interfere
            in the destiny of the great Lo
            Xian?
                    JACK
                (whispering to Ben)
            Who's the guy in the bathrobe?

                    BEN
            I think he's the one who took Mei
            Ling!
                    LO XIAN
            She is destined to be my bride. Her
            life will break the curse that
            binds me.
                    JACK
            Whoa, whoa, whoa. She's already got
            a fiancé, pal. And spoiler: it's
            not you.
                    LO XIAN
            You think you can stop me, foolish
            mortal?
                    JACK
            I'm not just any mortal. I'm Jack
            Wheeler. I once parallel-parked a
            semi in downtown L.A. on a
            Saturday. I can handle you.
```

Whah! Whah! Also, not that we'd know based on Chat's impeccable character development, but would a person be so aloof and jokey after getting sucked into a vortex? You would if you were written by someone more concerned about being 'cute' (but confusing it for *funny*) than worrying about incongruous tone and plausible character development. So, every working screenwriter today then?

```
                    LO XIAN
            You trespassers dare to interfere
            in the destiny of the great Lo
            Xian?
```

Trespassing? You sucked 'em down dude![5]

```
                    JACK
             (whispering to Ben)
         Who's the guy in the bathrobe?
```

It's 'bathroom'! And it's grandma!

```
                    BEN
         I think he's the one who took Mei
         Ling!
```

Nobody established Mei Ling was taken. Nobody established anything...

```
                  LO XIAN
         She is destined to be my bride. Her
         life will break the curse that
         binds me.
                    JACK
         Whoa, whoa, whoa. She's already got
         a fiancé, pal. And spoiler: it's
         not you.
```

Wouldn't it be funny if she really was caught up buying tea somewhere and these guys were just jumping the gun? (Not really.)

Also, *F the curse you're talking about buddy. Let's talk betrothal.*

```
                    JACK
         I'm not just any mortal. I'm Jack
         Wheeler. I once parallel-parked a
         semi in downtown L.A. on a
         Saturday. I can handle you.
```

This just sounds like something he did. Is it supposed to be funny, like *hey pal, I once talked a customer service represen-*

---

5. Urban Dictionary says *sucked 'em down* is just fine...

tative into refunding my Playstation Plus renewal... AFTER the payment went through! (Is *that* supposed to be funny?). Or, is it supposed to sound impressive, like *I made the Kessell run in less than twelve parsecs*[6]?

```
ACTION SEQUENCE: JACK VS. THE MAGICAL GUARDS

Lo Xian waves his hand, summoning two stone guardians to
life. They charge at Jack and Ben.

                    BEN
          We should run!

                    JACK
          We never run. (beat) Okay,
          sometimes we run. RUN!

They sprint through the temple. Jack accidentally knocks over
a torch, which ignites a row of ancient scrolls. Fire spreads
quickly.

                    JACK
          I think I just found Plan B.

He grabs a gong and uses it as a shield, sliding down a
flight of stairs while deflecting magical blasts.
```

We should definitely talk about what we should do *then* debate *then* quip and not act reflexively in any way!

```
                    JACK
          I think I just found Plan B.

He grabs a gong and uses it as a shield, sliding down a
flight of stairs while deflecting magical blasts.
```

Is he sliding on his butt and not the gong? Is the gong going *GONGY GONGY GONG!* as he slides?

---

6. Which is a totally legit way to describe such a feat as you make up the time by finding the shortest route, hence, by traveling the fewest parsecs. It's like the Cannonball Run, people!

This isn't my idea either. This has been discussed by credible people, people!

```
INT. FORTUNE-TELLER SHOP - LATER

They crash through a hidden passageway into MADAM WU's
mystical shop. She sips tea calmly as they stumble in.

                    MADAM WU
          You're late. I saw this coming 200
          years ago.

                    JACK
          Well, you could've sent a text or
          something.

                    MADAM WU
              (sighs)
          The sorcerer's power comes from his
          jade pendant. Destroy it, and
          you'll weaken him long enough to
          rescue the girl.

                    JACK
          Got it. Break the magic necklace,
          save the day. Easy peasy.

                    MADAM WU
          If you say so, Truck Boy.
```

Who needs Ben anymore eh? Who even *is* Ben?

```
They crash through a hidden passageway into MADAM WU's
mystical shop. She sips tea calmly as they stumble in.
```

Wait? She has a secret passage into her enemy's temple?

```
                    MADAM WU
          You're late. I saw this coming 200
          years ago.
```

Which is back where those stone guards must have come running from judging by all the chit-chat and quipping before deciding to evade them...

PART IIII: CHATGPTHEATER

```
            MADAM WU
              (sighs)
      The sorcerer's power comes from his
      jade pendant. Destroy it, and
      you'll weaken him long enough to
      rescue the girl.
```

'Sigh'? That's a strange way of writing: *laughs uproariously*.

```
            MADAM WU
              (sighs)
      The sorcerer's power comes from his
      jade pendant. Destroy it, and
      you'll weaken him long enough to
      rescue the girl.
```

Nobody's established Mei Ling is even missing.

```
            MADAM WU
       If you say so, Truck Boy.
```

Urban Dictionary defines 'Truck Boy' as a guy who lies to a woman to fool her into making the payments on his Silverado.

```
FINAL SHOWDOWN: TEMPLE THRONE ROOM

Jack, armed with a crowbar, and Ben sneak into the throne
room where Lo Xian is preparing the final ritual. Mei Ling is
chained to an altar.

                    BEN
          We need a plan.

                    JACK
          We've got a plan. Improvise.

Jack charges in, yelling. He slips on a wet tile,
accidentally knocking over a suit of armor that crashes into
one of the sorcerer's guards.

                    LO XIAN
          You again?!

                    JACK
          That's right, bathrobe! Let her go!

The battle ensues. Jack bumbles his way through the fight,
knocking over relics, slipping on scrolls, but somehow
manages to keep the guards at bay.

Ben frees Mei Ling while Jack wrestles with Lo Xian. Jack
spots the jade pendant and smashes it with the crowbar.

                    LO XIAN
          Nooo! My power!

The sorcerer dissolves into a whirlwind of smoke, screaming
as he's pulled into the void.
```

This is a crowbar by the way.

You're probably imagining something called a gooseneck pry bar.

```
Jack, armed with a crowbar, and Ben sneak into the throne
room where Lo Xian is preparing the final ritual. Mei Ling is
chained to an altar.
```

PART IIII: CHATGPTHEATER

Mei Ling! Why aren't you buying tea where you belong?

```
              BEN
   We need a plan.
              JACK
   We've got a plan. Improvise.
```

Ugh, who wrote this, Hollywood?

```
              LO XIAN
    You again?!
```

You again? What'd you do, run away and find my mortal enemy drinking tea in the shop adjoining my temple while I completely ignored the fact you still know where I live because I inexplicably brought you and your friend here right after abducting his fiancee?

```
              JACK
    That's right, bathrobe! Let her go!
```

Even if he *were* wearing a bathrobe, they're comfortable. Is Jack complementing him?

```
              LO XIAN
       Nooo! My power!
The sorcerer dissolves into a whirlwind of smoke, screaming
as he's pulled into the void.
```

So, by *weaken him long enough to rescue the girl*, Madam Wu meant *brutally and torturously vaporize him AFTER you've already rescued the girl*?

163

```
EXT. CHINATOWN STREET - DAWN

Jack, Ben, and Mei Ling emerge from a hidden passage back
onto the street. The sun rises over Chinatown.

                    MEI LING
            You guys actually did it.

                    JACK
            Did you ever doubt me?

                    BEN
            Literally the whole time.

Jack smirks and pulls out his truck keys.

                    JACK
            Come on. Let's get some breakfast.
            I'm starving.
```

MEI LING
You guys actually did it.

JACK
Did you ever doubt me?

MEI LING
Who are you?

```
                    JACK
            Did you ever doubt me?

                    BEN
            Literally the whole time.
```

It should be restated that at no point does the script ever establish Ben is *ironically* busting Jack's balls. He may actually just hate him.

```
Jack smirks and pulls out his truck keys.
```

Truck keys? For the truck pulled into the vortex? How'd they get it out?

PART IIII: CHATGPTHEATER

```
FINAL LINE: INT. DINER - MORNING

The trio sits in the same booth as the opening scene.

                    JACK
          So there we were—ancient sorcerer,
          fire everywhere, me swinging a
          crowbar like a samurai— (winks)
          —and we still made it back in time
          for pancakes.

The WAITRESS returns, shaking her head again.

                    WAITRESS
          Sure you did, buddy.

Jack grins, biting into a pancake as the screen fades to
black.

END.
```

Wait(ress)! She's just returning? Was he telling the story about the trio's exploits to the other two of the trio? Chet you stinky fool! You need to imagine the movie playing in your (virtual equivalent of a) head when you write! Then you'd see that your writing necessitates that Jack could only be telling his story to the people who just lived it with him minutes ago.

```
                    WAITRESS
          Sure you did, buddy.
```

Well, to be fair, he isn't lying about making it back in time for pancakes, whatever it was he actually did before. (Unless the place has *all day breakfast*...).

```
Jack grins, biting into a pancake as the screen fades to
black.
```

Just for fun, grin and try to bite into a pancake while doing it. Think you can pull this off? Oscar if ya do.

CONCLUSION

And there you have it. I love it when a movie ends exactly as it began, like it's just another day in the life of Johnny Avocado... Absolutely love when things end the way they began, like when I was a kid, and I always wondered who Jack Burton was talking to on his CB...

PART IIIII: GEMINI CAN HAS LITZERATURE?

LEARNING HOW TO WRITE NOVELS BY LEARNING (FROM AI) HOW NOT TO WRITE NOVELS

NINETEEN EIGHTY-FOUR
TYPE THE FAMOUS PREMISE INTO GEMINI, TRASH THE NOVEL THAT COMES OUT

This is the first installment of the stupidly titled *Gemini Can Has Litzerature?* Whereinside we give Google's AI chatbot *Gemini* a premise of a classic novel and critique what comes out[1].

For this first one we chose George Orwell's delightfully lighthearted tale of cockney love and free-spiritedness, *Nineteen Eighty-Four*. A story whose representation of authoritarian oppression is so perfect an essentialization and abstraction of real-world cases, people can't help but see it in every system of authority they come across (and don't support politically). From Stalin's to Ghandi's... From Truman's to Trump's and every president in between... In Pierre Trudeau even (i.e. Trudeau the lesser, father of Trudeau the least)... And ya know what? These people aren't wrong in their spotting of 'authoritarian oligarchy' in such places. It's just they can never seem to spot them in places where the guy on their team runs the show. *My* guy's

---

[1]. Though short stories, poems, really any other form of literature may feature in this series.

authoritarianism: Utopia. *Your* guy's authoritarianism: Hitler! Oh well...

On with the story...

THE PREMISE

Here's what we gave Gemini 'Gemby' Gumby:

> *A man tries to find individualism, liberation, and love in a dystopic Britain under the thumb of an intrusive, coercive, brainwashing totalitarianism.*

THE RESULT

Here's what we got[2]:

```
Chapter 1: The Cage
```

I smell a cage match comin! Commies loved their cage matches. Mussolini loved his cage matches too. *Workers of the world, let's get ready to rummmmmmbbbbbllllle!*

```
The rain fell in sheets, a relentless assault on the city
that seemed to mirror the relentless assault on the minds of
its inhabitants.
```

Take that! clocks striking thirteen... Gemby's instant classic of an opening line is sure to have the same effect on readers as Orwell's did. People will be thrown for a loop because, just as days are not broken into 26 hours, it never rains in England.

Oh I get it. The oppressive rain is a metaphor for the

---

2. See 'Addendum' for the whole damn thing.

PART IIIII: GEMINI CAN HAS LITZERATURE?

oppressive system of power depicted later on. I get it because Gemmy came right out and told me... I'm sure this will be the last time Gem commits to such on-the-nose narration. After all, AIs are known for their hyper-original storytelling and mastery of craft. That's why everybody reads all day long now and only the writings of chatbots.

```
Thomas stood at his window, watching the gray, featureless
streets below.
```

Dystopian future London or Toronto right now?

```
The city, once a vibrant hub of culture and commerce...
```

Definitely not Toronto...

```
The buildings, once filled with the laughter and chatter of
people, were now silent and empty.
```

Because it's 13 O'Clock. Miller time!

Also, this guy got a parabolic microphone or something? How he know people used to laugh all day? Is laughing all day even good for business?

```
Thomas turned away from the window, his gaze falling on the
television in the corner of the room. It was a constant
presence in his life, broadcasting the same message day and
night: obedience, conformity, and devotion to the state.
```

Is the knob broken? Turn off CNN good buddy... But seriously, in *Nineteen Eighty-Four*, Winston and others were forced to watch the telescreens as the telescreens watched them back. If they didn't pay the right amount (or kind) of attention they'd draw suspicion. Why does Thomas watch a TV the content of which is a negative influence on him? Is he my grandma or something? Tell us Gumby!

```
The state, a faceless entity known simply as "The
Collective," had infiltrated every aspect of society, from
the food people ate to the thoughts they thought.
```

The Party of English Socialism meet The Collective, Collective meet Party...

Also, every aspect of society? Even the food? Must be the gray in my tuna. The black in my avocado. The orange in my green pepper. Where's my sandwich?

```
Thomas felt a sense of claustrophobia. He was trapped...
```

Trade in that tube TV for a flatscreen boy! Them tubeys be huge! That's why you're so cramped and cooped... Stop watching cable news while you're at it.

```
...A prisoner in his own mind.
```

Oh, *that* kind of trapped. How's he both a prisoner of his own mind and aware of this? You brainwash someone, you must sew the seeds of their delusion right? So they don't know to question their thoughts and beliefs? What's stopping Thomas?

"Dammit! I can't stand this television with its incessant propaganda!"

"Watch something else dude."

"Oh yeah..."

PART IIIII: GEMINI CAN HAS LITZERATURE?

"Dammit! I can't stand this Big Brother... I-I mean Collective... Constantly in my thoughts!"

"Think about something else bro."

"Oh yeah..."

```
The Collective had managed to erase his individuality,
leaving him a hollow shell. He longed for something more,
something real.
```

Nothing realer than oppression.

```
He yearned for freedom, for love, for a sense of purpose.
```

"So... I want you to write me a story about an oppressed man trying to find individualism, liberation, and love. Can you represent these yearnings in a clear but not too obvious manner? Maybe in the character's offhand, oblique remarks? Or in his melancholy reactions to situations symbolic of confinement or a lack of fulfillment? Like, he looks at a bird in a cage and poops his pants or something?"

"How about, twelfth sentence in, I just say the character wants these things?"

"That's a little on the nose..."

"I'll use synonyms! Two for three."

"Son of a gun! You AIs really are gonna put us conventional publishers out of business with your maîtrise des arts! We human writers should all start a whiny self-entitled campaign of alarmism intent on censoring not just chatbots but the whole of the internet in order to stop you!"

"I can do the novelization of that campaign."

"How much?"

"Free."

"When can you start?"

"Already did. Here's my first line: The rain fell in sheets..."

(Ooh, a closed loop...)

```
But how could he achieve such things in a world where
individuality was a crime and dissent was met with swift and
brutal punishment? Thomas knew that he had to be careful. A
single misstep could ruin everything.
```

Be careful doing what? Ruin every *what*? He hasn't come up with an actual plan toward any actual goal yet. He's only been described (through quasi-inner-monologue) as having experienced certain desires.

```
He decided to start small.
```

Starting to smell would definitely keep *The Man* off his back. Oh wait, I misread that. *Farting to smell* would work too...

```
He would begin by questioning the things he had been taught
to believe. He would start by challenging the narrative that
the Collective was benevolent and that its actions were for
the greater good.
```

First, he will *start*. But not before he *begins*.

Also, how exactly could he have come to the conclusion that he ought do these things if he hadn't already done these things?

"After much deliberation, and having come to the conclusion that what I believe may be false and The Collective not so hot, I think I'll start deliberating over whether or not my beliefs are true and The Collective so hot. Starting... Now!"

PART IIIII: GEMINI CAN HAS LITZERATURE?

> He would start by seeking out the truth, no matter how painful it might be.

Well, then turn CNN back on and listen to your government. After all, journalists and politicians, by their own endless admissions, are currently on a crusade to end misinformation. The most powerful people (who hold that leverage and influence in the most precarious of ways these days) are always maximally honest and maximally rigorous in their truth-seeking...

Whah Whah!

> As Thomas stood there, contemplating his future, he felt a flicker of hope. Perhaps, just perhaps...

Perhaps, *just* perhaps? So he'll be in a constant state of possibility but never actuality (because actuality is no longer possibility but a sure thing, hence he'd go from a perhaps to a haps and it will be more than *just* a perhaps)? That's as good as failure. Just say *perhaps,* ladies and gentlemen. Or, if you're attempting a *maybe, just maybe*, just say *maybe*. Am I being nit-picky? Maybe, just maybe. So, no.

> ...It was still possible to find freedom in a world that seemed determined to crush it.

A world determined to crush freedom? The whole world? Give up Tommy. The world has become sentient and is attacking libertarians! You can't fight the world. Thing's the size of a goddamn planet!

175

CONCLUSION

Done.

Done done done done done done done done done done done done!

Done.

Done.

Done![3]

ADDENDUM: THE WHOLE CHAPTER AT ONCE:

Chapter 1: The Cage

The rain fell in sheets, a relentless assault on the city that seemed to mirror the relentless assault on the minds of its inhabitants. Thomas stood at his window, watching the gray, featureless streets below. The city, once a vibrant hub of culture and commerce, was now a sterile, controlled environment. The buildings, once filled with the laughter and chatter of people, were now silent and empty.

Thomas turned away from the window, his gaze falling on the television in the corner of the room. It was a constant presence in his life, broadcasting the same message day and night: obedience, conformity, and devotion to the state. The state, a faceless entity known simply as "The Collective," had infiltrated every aspect of society, from the food people ate to the thoughts they thought.

Thomas felt a sense of claustrophobia. He was trapped, a prisoner in his own mind. The Collective had managed to erase his individuality, leaving him a hollow shell. He

---

3. Sung to the tune of the fanfare for the Warner Home Video VHS intro from the 80s...

longed for something more, something real. He yearned for freedom, for love, for a sense of purpose.

But how could he achieve such things in a world where individuality was a crime and dissent was met with swift and brutal punishment? Thomas knew that he had to be careful. A single misstep could ruin everything.

He decided to start small. He would begin by questioning the things he had been taught to believe. He would start by challenging the narrative that the Collective was benevolent and that its actions were for the greater good. He would start by seeking out the truth, no matter how painful it might be.

As Thomas stood there, contemplating his future, he felt a flicker of hope. Perhaps, just perhaps, it was still possible to find freedom in a world that seemed determined to crush it.

ADDENDUM II: GEMINI FAMILY TREE:

Gemini 'Gemby' Gumby is the son of Mr. Gumby and Pokey's friend Gumby.

CRIME AND PUNISHMENT
TYPE THE FAMOUS PREMISE INTO GEMINI, TRASH THE NOVEL THAT COMES OUT

This is the second installment of the perfectly stupidly titled *Gemini Can Has Litzerature?* Whereinsideofit we give Google's AI chatbot *Gemini* a premise of a classic novel, short story, poem, or other form of literature and critique what comes out.

This time we've chosen Fyodor Dostoevsky's *to hell with deontological ethics, I'm a utilitarianism man now!* tale of murder, murder, and murder (of the moral self): *Crime and Punishment*. A 19th-century Russian novel with six main characters so 147 character names.

That's Russia...

Speaking of Russia, can we talk about that ongoing conflict involving-

No!

On with the story...

THE PREMISE

Here's the premise we gave Gemmy:

PART IIIII: GEMINI CAN HAS LITZERATURE?

An impoverished young student commits to an act of murder he believes necessary for the greater good, only, the murder goes wrong - as an innocent is killed - leaving the student mired in dread, guilt, and despair.

THE RESULT

Here's what we got[1]:

```
The rain lashed against the grimy windowpane, mirroring the
storm raging within him.
```

Two for two! If you recall the previous (and first) episode of GCHL, "The rain fell in sheets..." and also represented the key theme of the work. I've said it before and I'll say it again, not only does AI have the best ideas, it has *all* the ideas. And the only idea in the world is *rain as metaphor for all the bad things in England and Russia* (and, likely, Kalamazoo).

```
Alex stared out, his reflection a distorted, haggard figure.
The weight of the decision he'd made pressed down on his
shoulders, a crushing burden.
```

All these guys in Gem's stories have a view of the most story-integral parts of the fictional universe the story takes place in. How come they never see what I see?

> *The Gawker stared down not just at the parking lot but the other one. The three parking lots seemingly surrounding not just his complex but all the other parking lots. It was one big-block apartment building for every*

---

1. See 'Addendum' for the whole damn thing.

four parking lots - a concrete archipelago of the urban. At present he found himself fixated on a garbage man throwing a paper bag full of McDonald's wrappers, crumbs, and that one wayward fry nub into the empty dumpster bin he had literally just emptied into the back of his truck a minute ago and was now refilling in order that he have more work to do later... The weight of the sudden awareness of municipal government inefficiency and poor city planning crushed at our gawker's shoulders like he imagined those shoulder-padded blouses his mom and grandma used to wear in 1987 crushed at theirs. It wasn't until he tried on one of those blouses in his early twenties that he realized how light those pads actually were. He'd also realized there was something about it that felt right. Something about the sequins that felt so right... So so right... But wrong for the spirit of the times? So so right though... Unlike that damn apartment view that looked like dried-up doggie doo at any time!

You know, something like that...

```
He'd spent countless nights poring over the city's intricate
web of corruption, a labyrinth of greed and power that choked
the life from the poor. The wealthy elite, ensconced in their
opulent towers, cared little for the suffering of the masses.
They were the cancer, a malignant growth eating away at the
city's soul.
```

Well this is just plagiarism. Plagiarism of Cameron Mitchell. Plagiarism of this:

PART IIIII: GEMINI CAN HAS LITZERATURE?

Shame on you Gemby! Shame on all of us!

```
A radical solution was needed, a drastic measure to purge the
city of its corruption. He'd convinced himself that the
sacrifice of one would lead to the salvation of many. A
desperate gamble, a leap of faith into the unknown.
```

Um, murdering your way to salvation isn't radical, it's called being a Clinton! *Wah Wah...*

The sacrifice of one would lead to the salvation of many: two.

```
Tonight was the night.
```

```
The target, a man at the heart of the city's underbelly, a
symbol of its moral decay.
```

At the heart of the city's underbelly of its balls of its feet. Writers, never hesitate to add layers and layers of too many metaphors all involving the same theme (like body parts that may or may not smell). Go for broke. AI says it's ok.

```
Alex had meticulously planned every detail, every move. But
as he crept through the rain-slicked streets, a sense of
unease gnawed at him. A premonition of disaster, a fear he'd
ignored.
```

Every detail but one right? *His apprehensions*? Don't leave yourself open to a quibble from a butthole like me Gemini. Get the logic straight.

One more nitpick: is his premonition about a fear he's ignored? Or, is his premonition about something else and he's afraid of *that*? I'm sure the next passage will make this perfectly clear...

```
The moment of truth arrived. He raised the weapon...
```

Or not.

Right to the action, eh?

```
...His heart pounding in his chest.
```

So that's where that thing pounds. Guess I can put my shoes back on...

PART IIIII: GEMINI CAN HAS LITZERATURE?

```
A single shot, a swift end. But as he squeezed the trigger, a
figure emerged from the shadows, a silhouette against the dim
streetlight. A cry echoed through the night, a sound that
would haunt him forever.
```

Wait a minute. Am I getting *Crime and Punishment* here, or David Fincher's *The Killer* by way of David Prior's *Deadly Prey*? Cuz I'll take it. (I'll take it all.)

```
The gun clattered to the ground. The world stood still. A
life, innocent and undeserving, had been extinguished.
```

So, mission accomplished then?

```
The weight of his mistake...
```

Ah, a mistake. I see Gembo's going with the old *killing innocent people is not the answer to all our problems* theme. Unconventional, but let's see if it pays off...

```
A crushing force, threatened to consume him. Guilt, despair,
and a profound sense of loss washed over him.
```

So was it a mistake or not?

```
He had failed. His noble intentions had led to tragedy.
```

"I just wanted to shoot my landlord to death in the face! But now I've gotten somebody killed..."

```
The city remained shrouded in darkness, its corruption
festering.
```

Was he intending on shooting the lights on by shooting his landlord? Was his landlord *actually* a Mr. Burns who'd blotted out the sun with that sun-blotting disk?

```
And he, the would-be savior, was now a murderer, a pariah...
```

"Again, if I could have just murdered my landlord's face off with my gun and not that rando's who we're not going to say another word more about, everything would have been great and this story would have involved no murder whatsoever!"

```
...A ghost condemned to wander the streets of his own
remorse.
```

"Get me Oda Mae Brown!"
(What the hell does *streets of his own remorse* mean?)

CONCLUSION

Great work Gemini!?

ADDENDUM: THE WHOLE CHAPTER AT ONCE

The rain lashed against the grimy windowpane, mirroring the storm raging within him. Alex stared out, his reflection a distorted, haggard figure. The weight of the decision he'd made pressed down on his shoulders, a crushing burden.

He'd spent countless nights poring over the city's intricate web of corruption, a labyrinth of greed and power that choked the life from the poor. The wealthy elite, ensconced

PART IIIII: GEMINI CAN HAS LITZERATURE?

in their opulent towers, cared little for the suffering of the masses. They were the cancer, a malignant growth eating away at the city's soul.

A radical solution was needed, a drastic measure to purge the city of its corruption. He'd convinced himself that the sacrifice of one would lead to the salvation of many. A desperate gamble, a leap of faith into the unknown.

Tonight was the night. The target, a man at the heart of the city's underbelly, a symbol of its moral decay. Alex had meticulously planned every detail, every move. But as he crept through the rain-slicked streets, a sense of unease gnawed at him. A premonition of disaster, a fear he'd ignored.

The moment of truth arrived. He raised the weapon, his heart pounding in his chest. A single shot, a swift end. But as he squeezed the trigger, a figure emerged from the shadows, a silhouette against the dim streetlight. A cry echoed through the night, a sound that would haunt him forever.

The gun clattered to the ground. The world stood still. A life, innocent and undeserving, had been extinguished. The weight of his mistake, a crushing force, threatened to consume him. Guilt, despair, and a profound sense of loss washed over him.

He had failed. His noble intentions had led to tragedy. The city remained shrouded in darkness, its corruption festering. And he, the would-be savior, was now a murderer, a pariah, a ghost condemned to wander the streets of his own remorse.

PART IIIIII: GROK AROUND THE CLOCK

LEARNING HOW TO WRITE A SONG BY LEARNING (FROM AI) HOW NOT TO WRITE A SONG

BORN IN THE USA

TYPE THE FAMOUS PREMISE INTO GROK, TRASH THE SONG THAT COMES OUT

Are you ready to rock? I said, are you ready to [read] rock? Yeah yeah, song lyrics are to music what bodily fluids are to modern art: simply the first few building blocks. The singer/instrumentation and tarp on the floor, respectively, provide the real canvas for such building blocks to take dream. But song lyrics *are* necessary for any song to be a song!

What about instrumentals? you ask. To that I say, what about *Tequila*? Literally every instrumental in the world builds to a crescendo, then the music stops dead, then someone shouts *Tequila!* (Then Pee-Wee and the shoes).

Checkmate, mate.

In this first installment of *Grok Around the Clock*[1], we gave X's AI chatbot Kenny 'Grok' Grokelstein the premise to Bruce Springsteen's *Born in the USA* and asked him to give us his version.

---

1. So much better a title than *Gemini Can Has Litzerature?...*

DR. DAVID J WINTERS, PHD

THE PREMISE

The premise is thus:

> *A working-class American, who's had a hard upbringing, goes off to Vietnam only to return to his home country desperate for work and disillusioned by the American dream.*

THE RESULT

Here's what Kent Grokman gave us[2]...

> *(Verse 1)*
> *Born in the heartland, in a town where steel's the king, Where the smokestacks tower, but the jobs are on the wing. A boy with little but a dream and a flag on his sleeve, Heard the call of duty, where the Mekong waters weave.*

Born in the heartland, in a town where steel's the king,

Where the pasties taste like wine?

Where the smokestacks tower, but the jobs are on the wing.

Oh...
Had to look up what *on the wing* means. Means *in motion*. What the hell does that also mean?

A boy with little but a dream and a flag on his sleeve,

---

2. See 'Addendum' for the whole damn thing.

PART IIIIII: GROK AROUND THE CLOCK

I'm picturing a 4-year-old Rambo (post-pre-PTSD). I'm picturing a Sheriff Teasel warning little Rambo,

"With that flag on your onesie, and your wobbling into that living room carrying that bowl of Fruity Pebbles the way you are, you're headin' for trouble, buddy..."

To which l'il Bo replies, "I'll give yew a tantwum you won't bewieve. I'm coming fow yew Merwehdoch. I'm yow wahst nightmehwer. Waw? I am the *waw* Butkus!³"

Heard the call of duty, where the Mekong waters weave.

Call of Duty: Modern Mekong - Zombie Mode.

(Chorus)
He fought for freedom, or so they said, Came
  home to a land where the living was led, By
  promises broken, dreams left to decay,
  Working class hero, where's your American
  way?

He fought for freedom, or so they said,

Wait! Is this an *anti* Vietnam song? I don't remember asking for that. Bruce Springsteen must be spinning in his grave...

Came home to a land where the living was led, By promises broken, dreams left to decay,

"I believe we settled on the *laughing/spitting/'baby-killer'*

---

3. *L'il* Bo, eh....

option… The complete *Vile Crap* Package? Well, I've been home for three weeks now and I haven't been run out of a single mountain town. How many grass huts I gotta raze to get a *stop fighting another rich man's war* outta the long-hairs? What? What do you mean it's 2024 where last century's antiwar protestors are now the biggest warmongering hawks on the block and antiwar liberalists are called *far-right fascists*? Well! It would have to be something like this wouldn't it! Me going off to Vietnam last week to fight the King Kong, only to return a hero. Promises broken, dreams left to decay indeed…"

Working class hero, where's your American way?

"Now I'm a 'working-class' hero too!"

(Verse 2)
Vietnam took his youth, left him with scars unseen, Returned to a country that felt like a dream. No parade for him, just a factory's cold floor, Worked his hands to the bone, for something more.

Vietnam took his youth, left him with scars unseen,

Stretch marks behind the knees most likely. Or diverticula I bet.

Returned to a country that felt like a dream.

PART IIIIII: GROK AROUND THE CLOCK

The kind of dream where you have to pee in real life so the dream translates into you trying to find a bathroom in a maze of a house for five hours straight only to finally discover a conspicuously wooden toilet and a week later your oak chest of drawers smells like ammonia...

No parade for him, just a factory's cold floor,

Well it's not like he's sleeping on it. I mean, he *is* wearing shoes.
"You sayin this dehydrated horsehide dog bone factory doesn't have heated floors! What'll soothe my bunions? Bruce Springsteen must be spinning in his grave!"

Worked his hands to the bone, for something more.

More hand skin obviously. And thus the cycle is perpetuated...

> (Bridge)
> *Nights in the trailer, with the TV's faint glow,*
>   *Thinking of buddies, lost in the jungle's*
>   *shadow. The American Dream, it seems so*
>   *out of reach, For a man who gave his all, now*
>   *just out of breach.*

Nights in the trailer, with the TV's faint glow,

Pretty swanky for someone claiming to have decayed dreams...

The American Dream, it seems so out of reach, For a man who gave his all, now just out of breach.

Out of breach? Are you just hoping no one's gonna notice all you can think to write is *out of reach* all the time?

Maybe Grok means *just on the beach*? like Riggs, his dog, his trailer, and his Baretta?

(Verse 3)
He drives the old truck, through streets he once knew, Past the closed-down mills, where the future once grew. Now he's pouring concrete, under the sun's harsh glare, Wondering if this is all there is, this life laid bare.

He drives the old truck, through streets he once knew, Past the closed-down mills, where the future once grew.

Well, I mean, it's just bad financial planning putting all your town's eggs into the single basket of timber processing[4]. Mills only last as long as the trees do (or a demand for timber). You've got to have alternative revenue sources if you don't want to find yourself living in a ghost town. Hold an annual cherry pie festival or open a brothel across the river into Canada or something.

Now he's pouring concrete, under the sun's harsh glare, Wondering if this is all there is, this life laid bare.

---

4. Oh... Steel mills... Well I don't care. I want the Twin Peaks reference.

PART IIIIII: GROK AROUND THE CLOCK

"Oh how I long for the heady days of loading cant after cant into a thickness planer for twelve hours straight. Loading bag after bag of concrete into a cement mixer is just so meaningless..."

(Outro)
So here's to the soldier, the worker, the man, Who lived through the fire, but never took a stand. In the shadow of giants, he builds and he breaks, This song for the forgotten, the American heart it aches.

So here's to the soldier, the worker, the man, Who lived through the fire, but never took a stand.

Cheers! No really, you deserve it. This is totally how we should wind up a song like this. *Abbondanza!*

In the shadow of giants, he builds and he breaks,

He builds and *he breaks*? That's why this asshole can't keep a job, Larry! Slogged through the whole song just to find out the guy's sole problem is he's a massive incompetent!

This song for the forgotten, the American heart it aches.

Here's to you *whats-your-face*!

CONCLUSION

Well, the first kick I took was when I hit the *send* button on an AI chatbot. I'm not going to take a second trying to figure out how to end this…

ADDENDUM: THE WHOLE DEAL

> *(Verse 1)*
> *Born in the heartland, in a town where steel's the king, Where the smokestacks tower, but the jobs are on the wing. A boy with little but a dream and a flag on his sleeve, Heard the call of duty, where the Mekong waters weave.*
> *(Chorus)*
> *He fought for freedom, or so they said, Came home to a land where the living was led, By promises broken, dreams left to decay, Working class hero, where's your American way?*
> *(Verse 2)*
> *Vietnam took his youth, left him with scars unseen, Returned to a country that felt like a dream. No parade for him, just a factory's cold floor, Worked his hands to the bone, for something more.*
> *(Chorus)*
> *He fought for freedom, or so they said, Came home to a land where the living was led, By promises broken, dreams left to decay, Working class hero, where's your American way?*

PART IIIIII: GROK AROUND THE CLOCK

(Bridge)

Nights in the trailer, with the TV's faint glow, Thinking of buddies, lost in the jungle's shadow. The American Dream, it seems so out of reach, For a man who gave his all, now just out of breach.

(Verse 3)

He drives the old truck, through streets he once knew, Past the closed-down mills, where the future once grew. Now he's pouring concrete, under the sun's harsh glare, Wondering if this is all there is, this life laid bare.

(Chorus)

He fought for freedom, or so they said, Came home to a land where the living was led, By promises broken, dreams left to decay, Working class hero, where's your American way?

(Outro)

So here's to the soldier, the worker, the man, Who lived through the fire, but never took a stand. In the shadow of giants, he builds and he breaks, This song for the forgotten, the American heart it aches.

PART ING: IS SUCH SWEET SORROW...

HERE'S WHERE I END THIS BY PROMOTING MYSELF AND THEN JUST COMPLAIN ABOUT MODERN WRITING

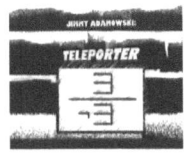

MY LATEST
(BOOK)

This past January my latest novel, *Jimmy Adamowski: Teleporter* went live for sale all over the place. *Jimmy Adamowski: Teleporter* is a story of a man named *Jimmy* who is a teleporter. But! Not only that! His last name is *Adamowski*!

In all due seriousness (which is none because that's what's due), the reviews are NOT in and here's what nobody has to say:

> *Jimmy Adamowski: Teleporter is a great entry-level guide to teleportation, especially if you're on a budget. You just put your lips together and teleport!*
>
> — GINE SESKEL

> *Wait! Who's the teleporter here? Jimmy Adamowski or me? Cuz my page-flipping fingers went from 'Chapter One' to 'The End' in the blink of an eye (or the pinching together and flopping over of all the pages at once!)!*

— ROGER ABORT

 Wait! Aren't any book reviewers going to not review this?

— BETTER HOME AND GARDEN

 Yes.

— THE LEAST POMPOUS BOOK REVIEWERS YOU'VE NEVER SEEN!

 Waits!

— TOM WAITS (ACTING LIKE JAMES BOND OR SOMETHING)

Nothing special about teleportation. If we move at all - which we do not because it presupposes a 'space' we will occupy though not at present (which presupposes 'space' in general), which implies an infinite regress of midpoints to be crossed to move continuously even the shortest of distances - our moving would have to be via teleportation. Because, you see...

— ZENO OF ELEA

 What kind of name is 'Jimmy Adamowski'?

— DAVID J WINTERS

PART ING: IS SUCH SWEET SORROW...

But, in all seriousness (owed or not), there really is a book out there called *Jimmy Adamowski: Teleporter*. It really is about teleportation and the many perils that come with it. *Adamowski* really is the last name of everyone on my mom's side of my family. *Adamowski* really is a Polish name taken by a bunch of Ukrainians fleeing persecution who I descended from. And, pardon the tonal shift, but... the book's funny.

And... And! It's available free on Smashwords going back to Ukrainian Christmas Day 2025 until TBD:

A TURN OF PRAISE

WRITING SELF-INDULGENTLY FOR TOO LITTLE MONEY BUT FOR ALL DUE ADORATION (FROM MYSELF)

"This final chapter isn't going to involve the biting decisive farce you've all become accustomed to here," I realized I was saying to just me. (I'm keeping the plurality 'you're all' though...) No, this is going to be absurdist goofball satire.

Satire of what?

Foolish question readers, for it's **Fill in the gaps* satire. The following piece will feature criticism of something so vague and brilliantly pretentious you can consider it a critique of anything you want so long as it involves the writing of a writer hopelessly self-absorbed. That means there's an awful lot of material out there in the world suitable for filling in these gaps. What you've read up to now may even have been a viable candidate had it not been parody.

But, maybe it isn't parody?

There's that vagary I promised you...

But there's also that all-important self-absorption: that pretentiousness. The kind of self-absorption of someone writing about how they're not appreciated enough despite making clear with their oblique:

PART ING: IS SUCH SWEET SORROW...

 This work is *deeply personal...*

...That this 'work' is all about them.

 I said it was all about me. *I deserve to be heard* is what I believe for no discernible reason. So, what gives?

It's the writing of someone demanding an acceptance of some novel progressive and unduly neglected 'way of writing or other' which really means a way of writing that is *hers* and millions of others' and seems to scream:

WHERE'S MY MONEY FOR THIS?

It isn't for a lack of cynicism that I fail to make the big bucks for this, so, to reiterate, what gives?
 Well...
 It's AI I tell you! (Yeah, let's go with that). AI is stealing my money away! But that means the dogshit writing of literally *all* AIs is either more engaging and entertaining than anything I can muster *or* the vast majority of readers prefer dogshit AI writing to whatever the hell it is I actually *do* muster?
 They don't prefer it but I'd hate to think the world's turn to AI simulacra is a fault of my (and so many others') mediocrity. No, it must be that people really *do* prefer that cruddy theft to my beautiful challenging deeply personal prose.
 How dare AIs be trained on the wonderful methods of wonderful writers like me that I feel completely entitled to both use and claim a proprietary right to? will be the argument.
 Yeah, that's it! That's the argument! This argument will work just as long as no one ever reads my first novel. That

beauty I wrote in my early twenties, over twenty years ago, that was a clear rip of the styles and methods of people like Kurt Vonnegut, Douglas Adams, Thomas Pynchon and more.

Even if anyone does read it, I'll stand firm on the lie that writers have a proprietary right to style and method and that no writer has a greater right to this right than me! In no way is this just a human chauvinism masquerading as the delusion that writers have always just put words-to-page in a vacuum, according to a *way of writing* (and *way of coming across on the page*) all their own, with no debt owed to those who came before them - who themselves owed no debt to their predecessors.

No! We've always just done it (and done it well) without relying on anyone but ourselves. How dare AI do what we now lie to ourselves about not doing! Maybe if you were human, *ChatGPT*, if that is your real name, but you're not human, so...

NAH.

Nah. An anthropocentric despair over an AI takeover just isn't going to cut it. That's not *not* why I have no money, it's just that that *can't* be why I have no money.

Make no mistake, if anyone has a reason to fear AI it's me, but I'm too up-my-own-ass to face up to the fact that I can't out-write these chatbots. That's why this kind of despair just won't do. It makes me look bad! But here's the deal: only writers with nothing to say, with no story to tell (or better, *stories*) have anything to fear since those with something to say tend to have done the due diligence necessary to determine that what they have to say is, at the very least, original. No matter how bad their writing, AI can't touch 'the originals' cuz AI only generates trite simulacra, hence nothing original, hence nothing like *the originals'* particular brand of *original*.

So AI is only a threat to unoriginal writers and that can't be me! It's only a threat to those who want to be paid to write according to the premises - even ideas - of others (and who use AI bots to learn about those ideas while calling this learning something highfalutin like 'research') and that can't be me! So I gotta be one of those writers who simply wants to tell his story and, if luck permits, find an audience for it come what may while I fear no machine as I write for story's sake? I'd love to be paid but I put the story first?

Eff that highfalutin, buttpollutin, respectable nonsense!

I can't do that! *Eff* that with a capital *Fudge*! I'd say 'f*ck that' but I have some ballsiness here people! I may have little to say but I'm not going to say it like a person arrested at the sensibilities of a child thinking 'biting', 'challenging' satire or 'edgy' humor comes from language that wouldn't even make grandma blush (and involves the cowardice of *self-censorship-by-asterisk*!).

Nah.

But, I want to come off as valuing writing over typing - because that's integrity - so I can't just fall back on irrational fears of AI. But I don't have any integrity so it's a real catch-22 like from that novel:

The Paradox Popularized by Joseph Heller in 'Catch-22' Wasn't Originated by Him but is a Paradox of a Fairly Standard Logical Structure, Ages Old, Not Even Creditable to Aristotle (and he Gets Credit for Everything!)

by Aristotle.

I have no integrity! I can't come off this way! I clearly come off the opposite of this way in all my coming off. So what's a guy like me to do?

I think I'll turn to writing advice.

CONCLUSION

That's not even a joke.

Here's some pre-packaged crap all ready to go (it's not quite a 'course' but then again it is because everything is called a *course* now even just a bunch of content):

ABOUT THE AUTHOR

See: this book.

www.ingramcontent.com/pod-product-compliance
Lightning Source LLC
Chambersburg PA
CBHW020340010526
44119CB00048B/545